39

An Open Letter To My Father

39

An Open Letter To My Father

KIM JACOBS

Hardback ISBN: 978-1-7363491-4-4
Paperback ISBN: 978-1-7363491-2-0
E-book ISBN: 978-1-7363491-3-7

Front Cover Image by Publisher.
Book design by Print Kreations.
Printed in the United States of America.

First printing edition 2021.
Purpose Not Permission LLC
309 Fellowship Road
Suite 200
Mount Laurel, New Jersey 08054

www.PurposeNotPermission.com
For booking inquiries,
email info@purposenotpermission.com

DEDICATION

To my late nephew, Jr; I tried and I miss you every day.
To my niece, Rana; I love you and I'm sorry.
To my late mother; you were right about everything. I didn't see it then, I know it now. I am beyond grateful to you for my upbringing, your tough love, along with all of your life lessons. Your display of grace, class and character is what I've always aspired to. I pray that I exude just an ounce of your essence.

You modeled unconditional love for others through the outpouring of your pure intentions. I've always and will continue to pour that out onto others.

You displayed true selfless acts of kindness by seeing and loving others as you love yourself. I've always and will continue to display that toward others.

You taught me the power of loving and forgiving others despite themselves. I will continue to love and forgive others who know not what they do.

Deep down inside I knew that it was time for your transition. Your outer shell could not withstand any more treatments or traumas. Even though I watched your health deteriorate while you lay in that hospital bed during those last six months of your life, I realize now that I was in denial. I simply wasn't ready to let you go. I selfishly wanted to keep you here, in pain, for me. I am now learning, through my healing process, that I did not know how to accept tragic loss. I now understand why the passing of your mother, my late Grandmother Sarah, was so hard on you.

You fought a good fight.

Your strength defied comprehension.

You are now at rest.

ACKNOWLEDGEMENT

I wrote this book because I made a promise to Andy, I am eternally grateful to you.

I am most thankful for my Creator; Father God. He placed these gifts inside of me long before I discovered them. Throughout my entire journey the signs were always there. As I look back, I now know why I've been spared; He simply needed me to be still to give birth to them. - Psalm 46:10.

To the entire Earn Your Leisure family; Creators Troy, Rashad and Matthew. Do you remember when I said that your creation was "History in the making"? I am so proud of you gentlemen. Thank you for all of the courses. You are all responsible for the majority of my success. I would never have learned all that I know about entrepreneurship nor would I have discovered the deeper meaning behind my true outspoken nature. I would never have found the courage to push past my fears by pursuing my true passions, my art. Thank you for creating your platform and for making it feel like a family.

Troy, fellow pisces, I still hear your words in my head "If you start a podcast, I would love to listen to what you have to say".

Rashad, fellow pisces, I still hear you saying "Everything is funny until it isn't".

Matt, thank you for showing me myself, otherwise this book would not exist. I am forever indebted.

To Nettie; thank you for your gifts, our random meeting, and for randomly suggesting that I go to check out Miss Ceily's Blues Venue.

To Faith; thank you for your gifts, for fearlessly pursuing your dreams, for birthing your brand and for providing a platform for creatives to unite by sharing our pain and passions through our art. Thank you for creating Miss Ceily's Blues. It's a warm safe space for all of us to walk in our purpose.

To E. A. there aren't enough languages to say thank you in so I chose English; thank you.

To all of the people who've destroyed me into the Woman that I have become today, I sincerely thank you. Whether you pushed me or pulled me, drained me or fueled me, loved me or left me, hurt me or helped me you were a part of my growth. You were all a necessary part of my process. Without you there would be no me. Some roses grow through the cracks in the concrete but the most beautiful flowers are grown through composts full of rotten eggs, debris and the filthiest mud.

To my father, thank you for fertilizing my mother's egg.

There is no Sun without the Moon.
There is no Light without Darkness.
There is no Pain without a Purpose.

You all helped me to discover mine.

Welcome to my Brand - Purpose NOT Permission™

CONTENTS

INTRODUCTION

This book was born out of necessity. I was triggered into writing it. I kept putting it down throughout the latter part of 2020 then I kept picking it back up as I heard Bishop T. D. Jakes whispering his messages in my ears "I Didn't Know I Was Me" "Believe" "It's Bigger Than You Think".

We make our own plans for our life while God laughs. This sentiment became so true for me that I had to get it tattooed on.
- Jeremiah 29:11

I never thought that I was "special" or "different" until the day that I realized I actually was. But aren't we all? We are all unique individuals with our own unique and individual experiences and perspectives. That's what makes our world united in its own beautiful way.

This book was a pain project, outlining my healing in real time. This is my personal journey outlined by my personal perspective told in my own unique way, using my own words. However, my story is universal. Everyone on this planet can find something useful in it to apply to their own lives.

There isn't one human being alive no matter your Race, Religion, Color, Creed, Class, Sex, Origin, or Socioeconomic Status, who hasn't experienced personal loss, tragedy, trial, error, pain, grief or internal upset. How we chose to process our truths and traumas is what sets us apart. That same choice is what determines the trajectory of our future. If we could all forgive ourselves first we can then get ourselves to a place of acceptance of what is, to then effectively deal with what was. We must all apply a healthier perspective to our journey. I pray that everyone reading this finds peace.

This is my guide to help you to do just that.

This is how you begin to do your work.

This is how I met myself.

FOREWORD

Life is a game of chess. It's a long, slow, deliberate journey as we all make each and every calculated move, one step at a time. Whether we actually know it or not we're all playing the game. Learning how to play the board game itself doesn't factor in at all. You can move left or right, diagonally, horizontally, vertically, backwards or forwards depending upon which piece you pick up. Every piece symbolizes what you make of your life. You can choose to not play the game by simply allowing life to happen to you. Or you can choose to make decisions that allow life to happen for you by learning to play this game in order to win. It's your personal choice either way.

What will you decide?

Is it checkmate?

Or is it your move?

INSPIRATION

This book was inspired by the album "4:44" by Jay-Z - Track "Adnis"

Letter to my dad that I never wrote
Speeches I prepared that I never spoke
Words on a paper that I never read
Proses never penned, they stayed in my head

March 1st 3+1 = 4
4 year old Trauma
44 years of unpacking

Do your work to begin your healing.

Chapter i – I Decided
My Catalyst of 2016

Level Number 9;

Where in the world do I even begin?

How much should I say?

Which words will be the most impactful?

Who am I actually serving by writing this?

When are our words inundating?

When are our words lacking?

Why does our unhealthy sense of pride and ego force us to believe that our perspective is law, and is all that matters?

Why does our healthy sense of pride and ego force us to believe that our perspective will somehow heal the world?

Where does our perspective meet its purpose?

The decision to sit face to face with you was birthed from my mother's passing in 2016. I decided to crawl back into the womb of my childhood in order to be re-born. I made an intentional internal decision to unlearn all that I was taught, in order to re-learn what was actually true about myself. I needed to make some drastic changes in my life in order to fulfill a promise that I made to my mother; She forced me to promise her that I would find happiness. I did not know at the time that there was no such thing. Happiness comes in waves.

Finding Myself;
It was an unearthing that I was not prepared for.
It was ugly.
It was brutal.
It was blood, sweat and tears.
It was war.
It took upsetting a ton of people.
It took upsetting and disappointing myself.
It took a ton of hard work.
It took discovering what was perceived as a beautiful monster.

In the end, I've decided that I am okay with being imperfectly perfected, shaped and molded by my parents, my family, my formative years, my upbringing after the storm, as well as every environment or room that I've ever stepped foot in. I decided that I would not allow any of the former to hold me back in my evolution.

I came to a crossroads. There was a missing piece. I needed to sit down face to face with you.

I decided in 2016, that I would no longer live my life the way that other people thought that I should. I decided to learn that "no" is a complete sentence and requires no explanation. I decided to say yes to me. Those decisions birthed my brand; Purpose Not Permission.

How to Say Yes to Yourself;

I would no longer exchange energy.
I would break soul ties.
I would break generational patterns.
I would experience solo travel, both domestic and international.
I would pour new, healthy energy into my mind, body and spirit.
I would only do what made me happy by placing myself first.
I would discover my purpose.
I would pursue my purpose relentlessly.
I would stop asking for permission.

I needed me.

I needed the authentic, unapologetic version of me, equally as much as I needed air to breathe. I made a decision that how I was living and relating with others was not working for me. I decided to change it, all of it.

I decided to change my surroundings by removing any person, place, or thing that was not healthy for me and my personal growth.

I decided that once I re-emerged, I would no longer allow any person, place, or thing in my life that was not working toward health or choosing growth.

I was not in a state of peace, so I decided to embark on a journey to find out what peace was. Happiness? Forget about it, what was happiness? I was at war.

How I Lost Myself;

My soul was dark.
My house was dark.
The energies that I chose to allow
around me were dark.
All of that darkness had infected
my soul.
That darkness tainted my heart and
my spirit.
It changed me into the lowest
vibrating version of myself.
I had to fight tooth and nail to
get back to my highest-vibrating,
truest-self.
I'd lost the music.
I'd lost my voice.
I'd lost my smile.

Even after this realization, I told myself that I had not known any better, but parts of that were a lie. I decided that once I uncovered knowing better, that no matter what, I would do better. In the beginning, none of this was easy. Once I dug into the action of doing my work, I deflected so much because the truth was such a hard pill to swallow. The truth of who I'd become and what I'd allowed was too embarrassing to admit.

However, this was only in the beginning. This was all before there was anyone else to hold me accountable, to show me myself. This was before I really knuckled down and decided to engage the mirror.

This was before my journey began with therapy.

This was before I ripped off all the bandages, took off the roller skates, removed the high heels, set aside the nice purses, and the cute outfits. This was before I washed off all the makeup, put on a sports bar, and strapped on the boxing gloves. Without distractions, I realized that I was in for the fight of my life.

Yesteryear;

In the past, when things got tough, I gave myself outs.

In the past, when things got tough, I opened the relief valves.

In the past, I lied to myself over and over because back then, it was the easiest thing to do.

In the past, I'd accepted countless others as they were.

In the past, I'd allowed others to assign their skewed perceptions of who I was.

In the past, I'd chosen to watch television programming which was a direct reflection of all of the normalized dysfunction, trauma, drama and chaos that I was surrounded by.

In the past, I'd accepted the diagnosis, swallowed the prescribed antidotes while fully embracing pain and hopelessness as normal.

All of that helped me to shape even more lies. The only way to get out from under the messiness was to ask myself some tough questions. How can you uncover the truth when your own vision is clouded? Why even seek the truth when your environment has shaped the need for you to believe the lies in order for it to sustain itself? What are you going to do about your truth once you uncover it?

Blurred Vision;

The lies are so much easier to live.

The lies are so much easier to tell.

The lies are easier to digest.

The lies are soothing, warm, cozy, comfortable, and familiar.

Blame shifting is far more entertaining.

Blame shifting is less pressure on ourselves.

Blame shifting requires zero work or personal accountability.

I was blinded.

How Sway;

If something is always wrong everywhere else and in everyone else, I escape all responsibility.

If something is always wrong outside of myself, then I do not need to do anything at all, inside of myself, in order to change my own narrative.

If something else is broken and I do not recognize that I am also broken, how can I lead?

If I refuse to do the work that is required to begin healing the broken parts of me, how can I have healthy dialogues, friendships, or relationships?

If there is no one there to hold up a mirror, and if I refuse to look in my mirror, then I have no work to do.

It gets really comfortable to coast through life dancing.

You are constantly toe-to-toe with like minds that will keep you on the dance floor of dysfunction.

All you have to do is keep the beat going, and keep on dancing.

Comfort zones are the keys to our demise.

Well, my feet were hurting, so I had to silence all the noise to learn a new dance. I had to break free from my comfort zone.

Accountability;

In the past, I allowed too much.

In the past, I made decisions that were not accurate reflections of how I was raised.

Those were the clear indicators of my unaddressed childhood trauma.

I was great at either adult displays of temper tantrums or suppressing my emotions.

I engaged conflict with conflict, which is a sure way to escape resolution.

I always thought that because of that, the war was external.

"They did this to me." "They said this to me." "They caused me to react this way."

The formers may both be true, the issues lie in the latter.

I needed the latter work.

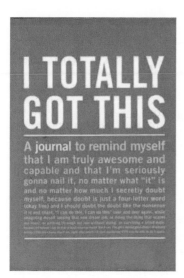

I TOTALLY GOT THIS

A journal to remind myself that I am truly awesome and capable and that I'm seriously gonna nail it, no matter what "it" is and no matter how much I secretly doubt myself, because doubt is just a four-letter word

Shifting Gears;

On my journey, I discovered that it does not matter what was said or what was done.

What always matters is if I respond, and how I respond.

It is so easy to point the finger, blaming everyone else for everything that's "wrong" with you and "wrong" in your life.

That way, you get to completely remove yourself from the equation.

If you are not the common denominator, then you have zero responsibility for righting any of your wrongs.

I had to ask myself. With that mindset, how exactly was my life going to change?

Doing My Work;

My first step was to completely withdraw from society to become completely still.

My thoughts then turned into non-stop journaling.

I purchased journals along with a great writing pen.

I began to write to myself until my trauma bled like cuts from a knife, through tears all over the pages.

Self Discovery;

Throughout 2017, I wrote about my life.

I began to process the story of my life and my emotional rollercoasters until I got to the point of the most beautiful realization.

It was all me, well most of it.

I discovered that the key ingredients to true life change were self-assessment, discipline, emotional intelligence and self-control.

I had to stop engaging in things that were dishonoring by removing myself from spaces where I didn't belong.

Put the Fork Down;

I also had to stop eating the things that weren't healthy, and stop watching television programming that didn't mirror the version of me that I wanted to manifest.
I have struggled with weight issues my entire life.
I was once 282 pounds, at my largest.
At that time, I did not like or know myself.
I would later discover that the people who encouraged my dysfunctional unhealthy weight did not like or know themselves either.
I had to put the fork down.
I had to push away from the whole table.

Absence of power;

The power to change my life was in my own hands.
I simply had to gain a grasp on my overall consumerism.
Your mind believes what you tell it.
I was more powerful than I'd ever believed.

Confronting myself has been the toughest, most demanding, challenging, tumultuous, painfully beautiful trip that I have ever been on. Prior to this, I'd totally forgotten what was important, what gave life its true meaning. Throughout this process of self-reflection, I discovered that conformity never worked for me, I always knew that. I always steered left as the world went right. I always knew that anything I did or was a part of had to be truly authentic to me and not just because everyone else was doing it.

I knew that I had a mountain to climb. I knew that this would be an uphill battle. I knew that I was going to have to face myself. I knew that I was going to be forced to deal with my truths and traumas. I had to challenge all of my beliefs while challenging my conditioning. I knew that I was going to have to upset a whole lot of people by saying no. I also knew that in the end, I would get to the other side of what was perceived as the beautiful monster.

I would meet a peaceful soul and a loving spirit.

I knew that for the first time in my life, I would be saying yes to me.
I knew that I would see and hear differently.
I knew that I would be viewing others as well as myself from much clearer lenses, an aerial view.
Those thoughts gave me butterflies.
I was excitedly terrified.
I had to set everything and everyone else aside to solely focus on me and my needs.
With intense pure focus, all of my tough decisions cost me the old me.

The no's expose so much truth.
You discover that everyone and everything meant to be in your life will stay.
Anyone and anything else will go.
There are some ties that you do not have to cut; those ties simply sever themselves.

My "to-do-list" seemed miles long; a complete overhaul that meant unpacking, exploring, and dissecting every single portion of my life with fierce intention guided by a great therapist, coupled with marrying a great fitness routine with learning about nutrition. It meant reading new books, listening to new podcasts, watching different television programming and learning what healthy dialogue within human relating actually looked like. This initial process of re-birth ironically lasted for a period of 9 months; the same amount of time that it takes for a woman to nurture a seed, then give it life.

Fully Committed;
I made a total commitment to myself, to choose me first each and every single day.
I made a total commitment to get up with a planned regimen every single day.

I made a total commitment to start each day with fitness and nutrition.
I made a total commitment to write every single day.
I made a total commitment to practice focused meditation every single day.
I made a total commitment to silence each and every single outside distraction in order to learn the real me.
I made a total commitment to decide to force myself into me.
I made a total commitment to create new, healthier, forward-focused, productive habits, while setting healthy boundaries.
I made a total commitment to become physically, mentally, and spiritually aligned.
It's a continual process.
It's called a journey without any destination.
It's every single day, and it's hard work.
Hard does not mean impossible.

Love;
I wanted to learn what true love was.
I knew that I was made of love.
I knew that I once was love.
I knew that I wasn't participating in love.
I knew that the only way to find true love was to, once again, become love.
I knew that truly loving myself was to study me by spending time with me.
I learned how to love myself.

Once you know who you are and whose you are, no one else can tell you who you aren't. I decided that I was worth it and worthy. I also began to understand that this is the toughest work that anyone could probably ever do in life. For that reason alone, most people don't do it. However, facing yourself is a lone wolf journey only achieved through solitude.

You vs You;
Until you study yourself, you won't ever know exactly what makes you laugh, cry, or what type of entertainment you truly enjoy.
Until you study yourself, you won't ever know what type of

energies you thrive around.
Until you study yourself, you won't ever know what type of energies bring your spirit down.
Until you study yourself, you won't ever know what you want to learn.
Until you study yourself, you won't ever know how you learn.
Until you study yourself, you won't ever know what your strengths are.
Until you study yourself, everything then becomes a weakness.
Until you study yourself, you'll never get comfortable with owning your weaknesses.
Until you study yourself, you'll let weak people tell you that you're weak.

You Can't Find it in any Book;
You won't know what direction you want your life to go in.
You won't be able to map out a satisfying life plan for yourself.
You won't know why you feel the need to poke, prod, judge, bully, or boss others.
You won't know why you gravitate towards drama.
You won't know why you're so entertained by war over peace.
You won't know why your knee jerk reaction to anything that you "don't like" is anger.
You won't know why drama is satisfying entertainment for

you.
You won't know why you cannot sit still and be silent.
You won't know why you need a drink or a smoke or a pill to lull you to sleep, or why without it, you're afraid of the dark.

Perspective;

Once you get yourself to this level in life, the pure psychology behind how the majority of society operates becomes a crystal clear lens to empathy. Once you get yourself to this level in life, you realize that the power that you possess is in you and your decisions.
You get to decide if you should react.
You get to decide when to react.
You get to decide how to react.
However, the ultimate level of power is in proaction, not reaction.

Once you get yourself to this level, there is almost nothing that you can ever be triggered by, offended by, or take personally.
Most situations simply require the application of a different perspective.

My mother's passing turned out to be the most traumatic experience imaginable for a multitude of reasons. It was also a beautiful gift in disguise. Had she not passed away, I would never have met myself by becoming this version of me.

I am still becoming.

Guarding the Gates;

God had to make me uncomfortable; otherwise, I would never have moved.
To say that I was extremely uncomfortable in my own skin and in my complacency would be an

understatement.
God forced me into action; he showed me that I had to
make so many moves.
I needed to uproot everything that was familiar to me.
I moved my physical location.
I moved my career.
I moved my life.
I moved my focus.
Everything and everyone else was left behind.
It's really easy to say that you're going to make drastic
changes in your life.
Actually doing so is a horse of a different color.
"Countless others want 'a different life' or so they think until
they find out the cost of it, until they find out what you lost
for it" - Ms. Lauryn Hill

Those words alone do not give proper language to the actual experience but that's the best way to describe how this journey started; so much has happened between then and now. Highs and lows. Ups and downs. Tears of joy, pain, struggle, and more tragic loss.

My head still wrestles with the need to make it all make sense. My heart and soul lean on my faith for guided wisdom and understanding. In the grand scheme of things, I do not have a single complaint. All of what I have experienced is exactly what was meant to happen.

Each hill of every growing pain gently guided me out of my comfort zone. Every peak and every valley served a very specific higher purpose.

Every laugh and every tear grew me into exactly who I was always meant to be, a much wiser, stronger version of myself.

It was all designed to force me to get comfortable with being uncomfortable. I cemented shut the doors of my past that were already closed. It all opened picture windows with scenic views into the land of opportunities, abundant blessings and countless possibilities. My steps were ordered by my creator.

We're now in 2018, once I shed the bulk of the weight, more fear

slowly crept in, so yet again, I had to be still.
I had to ask myself more questions…

Question is;
Didn't I ask God for this?
Didn't I set out to become the best version of myself?
Didn't I learn long ago that "Anything that's not growing is
dead?" - Ms. Lauryn Hill

Answer: Yes!

I still needed to sit face to face with you.

Chapter ii – David
My Trip Home to South Carolina - 2019

My purpose defied logic.

Initially all of the reasons for flying home to Columbia, South Carolina to see you were totally selfish, as I had every intention to be irrationally confrontational. In my mind, I envisioned the exact scene from the movie, "Antwone Fisher". Derrick Luke, a former foster child, having experienced a lifetime of trauma decided to embark on a journey of healing by tracking down his birth mother. He shows up to her home unannounced then proceeds to let her know that his life turned out amazing despite her absence as well as his brutal upbringing.

However, from our very first sit-down, you totally disarmed me. I'd completely reverted right back to being your baby girl.

Daddy's Little Girl;
The little girl, who loved you so much.
The little girl, who looked at you like you were her hero.
The little girl, who loved her father's laugh.
The little girl, who laughed just as much as her father did.
The little girl, who's chocolate skin tone was exactly the same as yours.
The little girl, who melted when her dad smiled bright and wide, while flashing his perfect white teeth.
The little girl, who remembered your quick wit, charisma and charm.
The little girl, who remembered making homemade ice

cream with you and who shared the same sweet tooth.
The little girl who adored you.
Deep inside I'm still a spoiled brat, a Daddy's Girl.

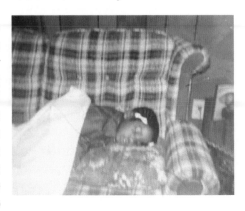

I was the little girl, who remembered our family's evening routine, as my brother and I set the table preparing for dinner; our mother would make the plates while you fixed your bowl of dessert. You would scoop your ice cream and cookies into a bowl, then place it in the freezer. Once we finished dinner, you went to town on it, devouring every last spoonful. You would then go into the sitting room to watch a little bit of television.

In your eyes, I was still the little girl who remembered sitting right next to you. My mother brought you a nightcap; you smoked your cigarette while we all watched television as a family. I reverted right back to the little girl, who fell asleep in your arms. I was the little girl again with pica, who ate dirt non-stop.

When I saw my father, I became the little girl who was banned from going outside. I had been caught far too many times eating the fresh dirt on the side of our house, so I was placed on punishment. The cravings had gotten so bad that I had to come up with a master plan. I started to sample the dirt inside of our house plants. I was apprehensive at first because the color of the soil was so dark. I was

used to eating the beach-like, light-colored sand outside of our home. I cannot recall how long I had been placed on punishment, but I do remember that the cravings were so strong that I was beginning to lose it. I went for broke on the house plant dirt; it was so good to me that I had gotten completely lost in the taste and textures. I was in so much bliss that I didn't realize that the huge chunk of "dirt" I was sucking on wasn't a chunk of "dirt". I do remember that I was trying to force it to melt. By the time I realized that what I was actually sucking on was a rock, it was already lodged in my throat.

I remember it being near the holidays, so my mother was doing her usual of cooking up a storm. Perhaps my brother was outside with his friends, I do not remember him being in the house. I do remember that I went from bliss to blue in about 3.9 seconds. I remember that I was hiding, crouched down on the floor under the table. To this day, I have no idea how you heard and found me so fast. I remember you picking me up by my ankles, turning me upside down, beating my back for dear life. I remember not being able to breathe, then suddenly, regaining consciousness. I remember that had it not been for my hero; I would not be here today. I remember my hero saving my life; more on that later.

I needed to see you face to face because I had so many questions. I felt, at the time, that only you could fill in some of the blanks in my life's story. I had already experienced a parent passing away, incredibly young. My mother had unfinished dreams, unmet expectations, unaddressed trauma and unhealed scars. I was left with so many unanswered questions and conversations that she and I will never have. I always told myself that I had time. Well, that time was violently cut short.

Over the years, I'd always known that I would fly home, specifically to see you, it was simply a matter of when. In 2019, there was a heightened sense of urgency. I felt that it was time. As my visit home to South Carolina neared, eager anticipation and nervous anxiety married one another. In essence, the plan was to play each day by ear. I simply needed to be certain that by the date of my return flight I would have everything on my "to-do list" checked off. I was sure that this would happen by simply following my intuition and moving how the spirit guided me.

I flew into South Carolina through Myrtle Beach. I'd spent a full week and a half on Myrtle Beach, but I was still playing it by ear. I wasn't sure which day I would leave the beach to drive up to see you. I am a self-confessed procrastinator; knowing that, I planned my vacation for a full month, being willing to extend my trip beyond that left me plenty of room to breathe.

On the beach I explored, I wrote, I read, I walked the boardwalk, I cooked, I listened to music and I danced. I met great people and I laughed, I laughed a lot. I meditated every day and every night. I slept with the balcony doors open, with my dog Bella-Angel by my side.

The ocean waves crashing ashore are the most peaceful sounds that you could ever fall asleep to. In the mornings I worked out, in the afternoons I walked Bella on the beach and let her play with other dogs. I met fellow animal lovers, booked full body massages, drank frozen daiquiris and smoked hookah.

I swam and spent time in the sauna. I laid out on the beach, taking naps while I tanned. I wandered, allowing my mind to wander. My mind would ponder over all of the things that I would say to you once I reached your front door. I never wrote down any of those questions, I simply prayed to God that our conversations would organically flow.

Expectations:

I prayed that I would get the answers that I was seeking.
I never blamed you for anything,
so there was nothing that I needed
to gain from you in order to get to
any place of forgiveness.
I simply had questions.
I never held any grudges against
you.
I just had questions.
My mother never raised her
children to despise their father.
My mother encouraged our

communication with you on countless occasions, over many years.
"Reach out to your father".
"Call your father".
"Develop a relationship with your father".
I finally made a decision to do just that.
I had questions.
I expected honest transparent answers.

I wanted to know why you never reached out to us. I wanted to know why the only time you and I communicated was when I initiated contact. I wanted to know why you continually made up so many excuses, inventing so many stories as to why it wasn't possible to develop a true bond with us, as teens or even adults, having our own personal telephone lines to communicate directly with us. As kids, we never knew your side of the reason why you guys separated then ultimately divorced. I had questions. I honestly wanted to hear your answers.

As adults, we heard the stories from plenty of other perspectives. I wanted to hear your story. I'd rationalized long ago that just because you failed as a husband didn't mean that you never loved us and didn't try, at first, to be a good father. Those are two separate responsibilities.

The Storm;
I remember the rain.
I remember the custody
agreement.
I remember the thunder.
I remember the split time.
I remember the storm.
I remember the child support.
You were gone.
You rocked the boat.

Despite all of that, our mother never displayed bitterness toward you in her heart nor in her spirit.

A Woman Refusing to be Scorned;

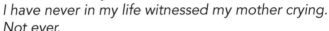

She never pumped us with rage.
She never poured poison into us.
She never said a single bad word
about you.
Not ever.
She loved you until the day that she
died.
She never changed her last name.
She made it no secret; she still
referred to you as her husband.
It ripped me to shreds when she
said on her deathbed "I should have
never divorced your father".
I have never in my life witnessed my mother crying.
Not ever.
She refused to be bitter, she wasn't a woman scorned.
Although your chapter ended, she never fell out of love with
you.
Not ever.
Our entire family knew it, her brothers and sisters knew it,
your sisters knew it, your brothers knew it, her best friends
knew it and she made sure that we knew it.

My mother taught me the power of love; she showed me what true love was and she modeled unconditional love. She modeled those behaviors that have molded who I am today; however, that level of love houses great internal pain.

What I Thought I Needed;

I needed for you to look me in my
eyes.
I needed for you to hear it.
I needed for you to know it.
I also needed for you to make me a
promise.
I have never asked you for anything.
We have never asked you for
anything.
You have never given us anything.
I thought that I needed you.

After two weeks had passed, I'd honestly gotten to a point where I did not want to leave the Beach to take the drive up to Columbia, but I'd made a personal commitment. My ask was more important than my peace. I knew that I needed to tread lightly. I knew more than ever before that I needed to be in the best frame of mind. I knew that you had a temper. I knew that if my approach was off-center, I could trigger you. I wanted to be certain to effectively and calmly articulate what I was feeling. I needed for you to feel the urgency of my immediate need.

My Why;
Over time, the initial meaning has become so diluted.
Over time, I've embraced the notion that we make plans while God laughs.
You and I both know now that my why no longer matters.

At the time, only two people knew that I'd planned to fly home to see you. Aunt Lois was one of them. I purposely never called you to say a word nor did I want to alert too many family members for fear that you would find out. Had you been alerted ahead of time my whole plan would have been ruined, our meeting would not have been organic. I planned to simply show up at your front door and let God move how he saw fit. That's exactly how this has all played out.

Manifesting;
One full year prior to my trip, in 2018, I randomly reached out to Aunt Sherry to make sure that your address and telephone number were still the same.
It was the day after I'd had a random telephone conversation with Mrs. Geraldine.
I wrote it all down, then tucked it away, not ever realizing the magnitude.
At that time I had no plans to come see you.
My spirit manifested it without my full awareness.

Once I landed in Myrtle Beach, there wasn't actually any concrete plan or any major details, I knew that I needed just a few small things to happen. I knew that I'd be traveling for an extended period of time, for that reason Bella-Angel was coming with me. That meant that I needed to research how she could affordably fly with me and what those exact procedures were. That also meant researching pet-friendly hotels, pet-sitting and a good dog groomer. I also knew that I'd need to rent a car. This presented some challenges because I was also traveling with an almost non-existent budget. I knew that my trip would be twofold, so I booked my stay in Myrtle Beach for the entire duration. I was planning to drive back down to Myrtle Beach afterwards to finish out my vacation, then I'd fly home from Myrtle Beach Airport. Once I arrived in Columbia, I had to double book another pet-friendly hotel for the entirety of my stay. You never offered me one red nickel and I never asked.

While planning my trip, I envisioned a room on a top floor that had a balcony overlooking the ocean. I knew that it had to be a decently-sized room because whenever I travel, the level of overpacking is beyond ridiculous. I probably packed twenty pairs of shoes that needed their own suitcase. I am extremely spontaneous, so I wanted to be equally prepared with dresses and heels as well as beach attire, casual wear, sports attire and workout gear.

Finally, I knew that I would have to grocery shop to cook my own meals. There was no way that I could afford to eat out like a tourist every single day. This, in turn, meant that now my hotel room had to have a full kitchen, stove and a refrigerator. That is quite a tall order to manifest when your bank account is laughing at you. I made it happen.

Throughout my entire life, I am quite sure that plenty of people have wondered where my mind is; my bank account is always in the minus yet still I rolled around the city like "Your Highness". None of that ever mattered to me. I never did mind the little things. My present circumstances were never real to me. I always looked straight ahead toward the possibilities of what could be, never focusing too much on what actually was.

During this entire process of unpacking my life, I finally realized that I'd always manifested my reality. Before I had anything, I always closed my eyes and imagined.

Rose Colored Glasses;

I see life in color.
I dream in color.
I still love those rose-colored glasses.
They have kept me genuine.
They have kept me honest.
They have kept me true to myself.
Despite and in spite of, I'll never take off these
rose colored glasses.

I used to hold tight to the notion that I did not know who was protecting me, just knowing that we hit it off. I know now that was a lie. God was always there. His footprints were always the only ones in the sand because he has been carrying me this entire time.

Kintsugi;

There is something to be said
about being broken.
Being broken by others allows
room to show grace towards
those who have inflicted harm.
The broken are always more
evolved.
Those who seek to cause harm
to no one.
Those who see everyone as
they see themselves first.
Those who protect and cover
others.
Those who know all too well
what it feels like to never have
been protected.
Those who bother absolutely no one, except when forced
to aggressively defend themselves from personal attacks of
intentional hurt and harm.
Titus 1:15.
Being broken is better than being new.

When the Japanese mend broken objects, they aggrandize the damage by filling the cracks with GOLD.

They believe that when something's suffered damage and has history it becomes more beautiful.

You should know that I have also redefined the way that I view religion. That stance will continue to evolve as I continue to grow. As of now, I no longer believe in organized religion. I do not subscribe to any mortal man who is a sinner just like me pushing ideologies and doctrines down my throat in an effort to cast judgement. I do wholeheartedly believe in God. I believe in the parables of the written word. The scriptures speak to me in unnatural ways. I know that I am God's child, being used as a vessel to further his purpose, not mine.

My Belief System;
God keeps his promises; it is evident in the fruits of my labor.
I believe in paying my 10% in tithes and giving to those in need.
I give from my heart, not just for a tax write off.
I believe that life is about service to others through the proper balance and boundaries.
I believe that my purpose is to serve others.

In some ways, women are God, we bring much needed balance to the Universe with alignment through our feminine divine. More importantly, we bring life into this world. Without us, there would be no you, Sir.

I believe that God lives in our hearts and minds. I do not need a written rule book to teach me how not to be a horrible person to other people, my mother taught me that. I do not need a written rule book or a guide to teach me to love my neighbor as I love myself, my mother instilled that in me. I do not need anyone watching over me to teach me that if you have two, give someone else in need one, my mother demonstrated that. I do believe that I need the guided spirit-led word of God along with his protection. Without it, I am nothing. The peace that I have now shows me that I have always had God's protection. Religion is for those that are afraid to go to hell, while Spirituality is for those who have already been through hell and back.

There was a ton to accomplish on this trip. Once I got to South Carolina, I wanted to try to see as much family as I could. I planned to pay a visit to Uncle Bubba in Barnwell. Reggie and Q told me that he was extremely sick. It was important for me to give him his flowers while he could still smell them. I was devastated by the news of how sick Uncle Bubba was. Just three years prior in 2016, he and the boys piled up in the truck, driving

all the way up North to attend my mother's memorial service and to spend time with our family. For reasons outside of my control, they never made it to the memorial nor did they get to pay their respects to my mother but they honored her in a different way.

They made it their business to track me down. They spent a great deal of time at my home. We were all able to just sit around, talk and to catch up. We looked through tons and tons of old photos, laughing and sharing countless family memories and stories. The boys told me stories about you that I never knew. We all went out to eat at a local restaurant, then we drove down to spend time with Rana and Jr., my brother's two oldest children. Uncle Bubba and the boys had never met them in person. We all had a great time that day.

It was such an amazing feeling to catch up with them. Years had gone by since I had last seen them. Once the visit was over, it felt like no time had passed. Throughout all these years, my mother remained close to your side of my family. You two grew up together, your side of my family always loved her. Your mother, my Grandmother Rosalie, revered my mother. That is why, years later, when Grandma Rosalie passed away, my mother made it her business to pack us up in the car, to take that 12 hour road trip from Philadelphia, PA to Barnwell, South Carolina to pay our respects. We all drove down South to attend her funeral. We even brought my Grandmother Sarah along. I'm sure that you remember. I heard years later that you were upset by it. As if we did not have a right to attend our own grandmother's funeral. I find that to be particularly strange knowing that you stopped speaking to Grandma Rosalie many decades ago. None of your side of my family really knows Jenny, any of her family or the boys. You never brought them around. Weird, right?

My mother remained extremely close to Aunt Lois and Aunt Sherry. They were always sending photos back and forth, having telephone conversations that lasted for hours, while laughing hysterically about any and everything. My mother was always the glue. She remained close to your side of my family; through her, my aunts knew me.

In the years since my mother's passing, my aunts and I have become much closer. Aunt Lois and I have had long telephone conversations. She and I have a running joke. At random times, I'll think about it and laugh so hard that I cry real tears. It's an insider; although your actions are the origin of that joke, sadly, you wouldn't understand it.

Aunt Lois and Aunt Sherry tell me often how much they miss my mother. I most certainly understand why, her gut-busting laughter plays often in my own head. Boy, do I miss her laugh too.

Once I got to Columbia, I visited my elementary school, Satchel Ford, as well as my brother's middle school, Dent. I planned to visit our old church, Abundant Life Ministries, to try to track down our old Pastor, Sister DeBerry. But I found out on my trip that Pastor DeBerry died in 2005. I was shocked to learn this, she was only 58 years young.

I spent time with Ms. Shirley, my mother's good girlfriend whom I had not spoken to in almost three years. She and I went out to eat with Bella-Angel in tow. I learned that she is terrified of dogs. We broke bread and shared insane laughter as she literally would tense up and run every time my 10-pound fur-baby got near her. The last time that I saw her, before then, was in 2016 when she took the train up North to visit with my mother in her last days at the hospital. Ms. Shirley always refused to fly; she told me that she was terrified and had never been on an airplane. She often made trips up North to visit, always taking the train. Ms. Shirley and I spent a great deal of time together, I was happy that she was able to spend quality time with her friend before she passed away.

I spoke to Mrs. Geraldine, my mother's best friend, on the telephone often during my trip. They live in Texas now, ironically she and Mr. Marvin had been in Barwell, South Carolina just a week prior to my arrival, attending a wedding. I'd just missed seeing them by a few days. She was so excited to learn that I was finally at home visiting. Did you know that Mrs. Geraldine flew up North and spoke at my mother's Memorial Service? She and Mr. Marvin both attended. I told you that Mr. Marvin asked you to reach out to him, I now understand why you never called him.

Mrs. Geraldine and my mother remained genuine best friends and confidants from the time that you all attended grade school together throughout all of these decades of time, space and circumstances. She is the epitome of what a best friend looks like. I marveled over their relationship, always wishing that I had that.

House cola. S.c.

I planned to visit the three homes that my mother, brother and I lived in. The home that has the most significance is the home that we lived in after you guys divorced. I remembered the exact neighborhood, location and addresses of two of the homes that I went to visit; the third one was a challenge. I walked right up to the front door of our old home on Brenthaven Road. I remembered that address vividly because over the years those 4 numbers were my mother's password, which she used for everything. Thank God the new homeowners were black, God only knows what could've happened to a black woman in the South randomly roaming in a stranger's front yard.

I rang the doorbell and boldly asked them if I could come inside to have a look around. I told them that I was born in that house and that it held so many fond memories. I was kicking myself for forgetting to bring the pictures of our family

inside of that home. I have one specific photo that will forever be etched in my mind of me standing in the front yard in pigtails and a yellow shirt. That picture is the essence of who I am; happy, innocent, and carefree in full diva mode, with my hands in the air and a huge grin on my face.

I explained to them that I was traveling and no longer lived in Columbia, having relocated as a pre-teen. We spoke through a closed door and of course, as any sane person would, they kindly declined my request to come inside. So as not to seem totally insanely weird to them, I gracefully stepped away from their front porch and got back in my car. I took pictures of the outside of our old home and sent them to my brother. I will always have that memory.

Next up was Valleybrook Road. The memories in that house were not as bright and colorful, so I simply drove by, parked outside for a little while, reminiscing, and then drove off.

Our third home was the true challenge. I knew that it was on Dartmore Lane. I vaguely remembered the house numbers. I knew that it was somewhere near my brother's middle school, Dent, but I never found it. Through therapy, I've learned that that's where my memory lapse began. That house stored so much of my childhood trauma. Among other things that's where Matthew shot me in the face with his BB gun.

I vividly remember our mother opening our sliding glass back door that led out to our backyard, calling us in for dinner. We were outside

playing with some of our neighborhood friends, Phillip and Matthew. They were brothers, with Phillip being the oldest, going along with my brother in age. Matthew was the runt and he was a terror. He loved guns, I guess he took after his father. Their parents trained them to shoot at a very young age. Our backyards were adjacent.

Matthew had his BB gun, and had climbed up into their tree house to use me as target practice. I remember that an argument started and I was trash talking to Matthew. I was walking toward our house while trash talking with my back turned away from him. For a split second I turned back around to look over my shoulder, at that precise moment he pulled the trigger. His aim was immaculate. We had to have been at least 12 or more feet apart plus he was shooting on a downward angle. The shot landed on the right side of my temple an inch away from my eye. I still have the scar today. Needless to say that we never made it inside of our house to eat dinner that night. I do not remember the ride to the Hospital nor do I remember how many stitches I received.

I drove to that old neighborhood, found the street, then I proceeded to drive around and around for hours. I spent so much time trying to locate that house. I could not seem to get anyone on the telephone that could lead me straight to it. I spent the next day searching as well. As I think about it now, perhaps I never truly wanted to find it. Perhaps I wasn't really ready to face that trauma alone. That was the only home that I never got to. That house has so much significance and so much meaning. My brother and I both left so many scars there. We have had countless conversations about our memories there. I remember a lot from those times "way back when," but I did not remember that you'd never visited us there, picked us up, nor dropped us off at that home. When you told me that, I found it strange. I guess I have to take your word for it.

I told you to your face before I left South Carolina, and you and I have spoken about this countless times since; I want that house. I asked you to find it for me, and you promised me that you would. I know now that you were not sincere. I was not asking you to buy the house for me. I will figure that part out. I just need to find it. You seem to have a tad bit of difficulty keeping your promises. You seem to have a tad bit of difficulty with even telling me the truth, Sir. The end result of the trauma that you inflict usually costs someone their life. I know that it's a heavy cross to bear, but look over your track record, Sir.

Broken Promises;

I want that house.
You said that you would find it for
me.
Find it for me.
I don't care who lives there.
I don't care about the condition of
it.
I don't care if it isn't for sale.
I don't care what it takes.
I don't care about your excuses.
I want that house.
One day I will own that house.

I cannot ever say that I blame you for my childhood trauma, but your hands are not clean either. You have to look yourself in the mirror; I do not. You have to live your own truths; I do not. What you do on a day-to-day basis does not affect my life. I have rebuked and revoked those privileges, Sir. You do not get that satisfaction, Sir. What I would suggest is that you work with God, the true version of God, not ideologies, get some good therapy and figure out how to start telling yourself the truth. Perhaps that would lead to you forgiving yourself.

What Bitterness Looks Like;

In the end, when it is all said
and done, you have been your
own worst enemy.
Your entire 70 years on this
planet have been filled with an
underlying un-forgiveness.
You have never forgiven your
Father Albert, who cheated on
his wife, had an affair with your
Mother Rosalie, producing you.

You were born out of wedlock into dysfunction.
Do you not realize that a large majority of children are
produced that very same way?
It's your reality.
What is your real gripe?
Why are you still so angry and bitter?

 You don't know this, but I know that you went to see your father. Years after my Grandmother Rosalie passed away you sought him out to try to build a bond with him. I've heard the stories about the personal heartbreak and devastation that you experienced once he rejected you. I've heard that you had all kinds of horrific things to say about him not wanting to be a part of your life. Weird, right?

Trigger Warning;
Absent father's don't have the right to complain that their father's were absent.
Your resentment toward my Grandmother Rosalie closed your heart, in any real sense, with women.
You're an absentee father.
Your resentment toward my Grandfather Albert, whom we've never met, shaped the way that you've behaved with women and dictated your hardened disconnect with parenting.
Imagine an absent father having the nerve to complain about his father being absent.

You loved my mother in your head, not with your whole heart. You were never taught how to love her with your heart. From what I've observed, in your marriage with Jenny, I believe that you've still never learned how not to be guarded and to fully trust any woman in any real way. How could you? You were never shown how.

My Grandmother Rosalie was a beautiful spirit but she, too, was troubled. Her parents failed her. So, the cycle continues. Why aren't you embarrassed? The only person that you have to blame is you. The only person that can change you is you. Do you honestly feel like your dysfunctional disconnected behaviors today toward the children that you produced is normal?

The last piece of my "to-do-list" during my trip was to finally lay my mother to rest by spreading her ashes throughout her childhood home. Now, this was the real task and far superseded anything else that I planned to do.

I had to drive up and down the dirt roads of Barnwell, South Carolina and feel my way around to find my grandfather's home. I had no idea whether or not that home was still there, but I had to try my best to find it. Hard never means impossible; hard simply means applying more effort, so I took a shot.

My grandfather was Morgan Simon "Man Simon" to everyone in town and he left his mark. My Aunt Janice named her son Morgan, as an honor to her father. Man Simon was a local celebrity, almost an urban legend. In addition to the home, adjacent to his property housed his Juke Joint and his Farm. He raised hogs and chickens and had a curing house that he used to preserve the meat.

As children, we all spent lots of time with him and a lot of my cousins from my mother's side of my family, who were all born up North, visited his home. We knew our grandfather very well. We watched him ring chickens' necks and watched my grandmother pluck their feathers, clean them, then cook them.

My Grandmother Sarah would cook fresh eggs and bacon along with the best hot water cornbread. She scrubbed those floors clean, keeping a spotless home. She was a homemaker who was great at crafting and sewing while taking great care of my mother, aunts and uncles by making sure that they had everything that they needed and most of what they wanted.

 My grandmother could not read or write but she had wisdom that far superseded any level of formal education. My grandfather hosted pig roasts on any given night on an open fire pit. He would dig a hole in the ground and use an oil drum barrel to cook the whole pig. Everyone in town came to eat, buy his homemade moonshine, play the jukebox or pool, or to just shoot the breeze.

He had a convenience store, selling his liquor along with a variety of other things like jars of whole pickles, pickled pig feet, fresh peanut brittle and a host of other snacks. There isn't anything sold in stores today that even comes close to the tastes or textures of the food and candy from my childhood.

There was always a party with the music blasting while everyone in town gathered for amazing laughter and lots of love. I reminisced heavily over those days.

As I drove up and down those roads, I remembered the thick red clay that we would carve out on the side of the road which we ate as children. I also remembered my Grandmother Rosalie's trailer home where we spent plenty of time. We played outside in the yard, catching lightning bugs or dodging huge red fire-ants. Those were the type of ants that you'd step on, but they still wouldn't die. We would step on those ants to try to avoid being bitten, but they came back to life over and over again. Eventually, we would give up.

I recruited my cousin Q to help me find the property. I called him as I was driving down to Barnwell, telling him what my mission was. He didn't ask any questions; he simply told me to come pick him up. I pulled up and he and I were off on this journey. I felt in my spirit that if I could randomly find an elder on the side of any one of those dirt roads, I could simply pull over and ask, "Do you know where Man Simon's house is?" I knew that simply saying his name would

be the key to pointing me in the right direction. That's exactly how it happened.

Q and I found two elders shelling peas on the side of the road. It was blazing hot outside that day, so when we pulled up on the couple, they were sweaty and parched. It seemed that they had been outside for the better part of the day shelling those peas while just living their life as most southerners from the deep south do. There was no sense of urgency nor any real concept of time. As soon as I said the name "Man Simon" they both perked up with excitement. They were eager to help us out. I told them that I was his granddaughter visiting from up North. I told them that it had been many years since I'd visited home and that I had no idea how to get to his house. That was all that I had to say. They treated me

as if I was an heiress. Their high respect, admiration and regard for my grandfather showed in their actions as well as their demeanor.

The elders knew exactly who he was and where his property was. I asked if they would come along for the ride, they obliged without any hesitation. They put their peas away, packed up their pocket knives, hopped in my rental and we were off. We stopped by a local town store so that I could buy them beer and snacks. At the same time, I also found out that my cousin Q speaks Spanish. I speak just enough to get by, but I learned of his skill by hearing him have fluent conversation with the Store Owner. I was shocked to learn that the local store owner nor the clerk were native Southerners.

The South that I'd known and loved has changed so much.

It turns out that Q and I had actually done a good job of getting pretty close to my grandfather's property, we found ourselves to be about five minutes away from where we picked the elders up. As I was driving, the elders were telling us stories that brought back so many amazing memories. They knew so much about my family, more than I'd ever known. They told us stories from their perspective, while we listened intently or laughed wildly at their jokes. They told me that my grandfather died right in his front yard and that the locals would later dig up the ground searching for buried moonshine and money. The only part of that story that I questioned in my mind was where he actually died.

When we reached our destination, I was floored to find out that the house was still standing. The curing house and the outhouse in the back were gone; so was the Juke Joint next door, but that tiny two bedroom home was still there.

There were tons of weeds, tall grasses and debris. There was an unkept outer shell with broken front steps but the foundation of the home was as strong as ever. The walls of that home housed the very essence of who I am. The walls of that home marked the beginning stages of everything that I have become thus far and everything that I am becoming. The walls of that home housed and birthed greatness through instinctual survivors skills, talents and gifts. However, the walls of that home housed far too many secrets, trauma and pain.

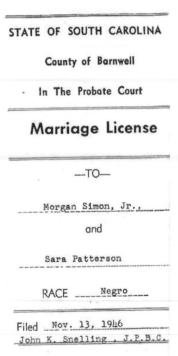

STATE OF SOUTH CAROLINA

County of Barnwell

· In The Probate Court

Marriage License

—TO—

Morgan Simon, Jr.,

and

Sara Patterson

RACE _____Negro_____

Filed _Nov. 13, 1946_____

John K. Snelling , J.P.B.C.

My Grandfather Man Simon, married my Grandmother Sarah Patterson, giving birth to my Mother Lou Ethel. My Grandmother Sarah had twelve pregnancies, birthed ten children but raised eight survivors. My Grandmother Sarah had two miscarriages and two of her children passed away as babies, one presumed to be from crib death. My grandmother and grandfather together raised six girls and two boys, the eldest being my Uncle Richard, the youngest, my Uncle Rodney. My mother, along with all of my aunts came in between.

Next to my mother, my Grandmother Sarah was the strongest woman that I have ever known. She allowed my grandfather to lead by being the man of the house. Man Simon was the provider and the protector and would do anything for his family. That is why his nickname was "Man". However, he also had a wandering eye that wandered over to many women throughout those years.

All told, Morgan Simon has approximately twenty five or more children by at least four different women. My grandmother eventually had enough of his infidelity, so one night she decided to pack up her eight children, leaving him for good. My grandmother migrated North years prior to us, to one of our distant cousins' homes so that she could start a new life for herself by showing her children something better. She had no idea what living up North would entail but she knew that she and her children deserved to live in a healthier environment surrounded by love and support.

She decided to stop tolerating her husband's blatant disrespect.

Yes, Man Simon loved his family while being a dedicated father, but he seemed to love embarrassing his family equally as much. Barnwell is a very small town and my grandfather was a very prominent figure in it. Everyone knew his name simultaneously, everyone feared him. The town regarded my Grandmother Sarah as well as her eight children as the first family. However, everyone also knew about his infidelities and his children birthed from his mistresses. Leaving him was the best decision for her to have made. Had she stayed, he would have ruined her.

As soon as I walked into that home, I could feel the love and the pain that was left inside. Those emotions were thick. They were etched into the floorboards, the ceilings and the walls. The love and the pain was deeply rooted in the wood. There was a lone piece of furniture still left inside, a small wooden chest with legs, pull out drawers and cabinet-like doors that opened up. I pulled out the metal casing that held my mother's ashes and proceeded to open it so that I could leave her essence behind.

It was honestly the first time that I really took a good look at the metal outer-shell of her urn. I had the hardest time trying to get it open, as I had no idea that it was basically cemented shut. The elder gentleman pulled out his pocket knife and used every ounce of his strength to pry it open. That wasn't working so his wife, the elder woman, and I searched from room to room trying to find some sort of random tool to use. Q was instinctively filming videos, but eventually, he put the

camera down as all four of us were now on a mission to pry open my mother's urn.

We finally got it open. We all breathed a sigh of relief. My tears began flowing as I looked down at my mother's remains.

Throughout the many years of living up North, through my mother's beautiful transformation and her life's incredible journey, one thing was always a constant; my mother was a Southern woman who held onto the morals and principles of her upbringing. Her rearing was rooted in Southern culture and she always wanted to come back home. I knew that by spreading her ashes all over the home that she was born and raised in and by leaving her gold metal urn neatly packed away inside of that lone piece of wooden furniture, I was doing the right thing. I knew that my mother's unspoken words, her unhealed wounds along with all of her unaddressed childhood traumas would finally be resting in peace.

As we packed up to leave, I took countless pictures of the inside of that house. I closed my eyes and imagined the years that my family spent there. Ten people living inside of this tiny home who had no idea that they grew up poor; eight children who were provided for and given the best of everything that life had to offer them; eight children who  never went hungry, having home-cooked, delicious Southern meals made from scratch daily; eight children who were sent to school fresh and clean every day in good sturdy shoes and the best of the linens that my grandmother had hand-sewn and hand-washed.

 A married mother and a father raised eight children as a family in a clean house that smelled like fresh pine. A family who was taught to stick together, protecting and defending one another from neighborhood bullies, anyone or anything else that would try to divide or tear them apart. I am forever grateful to those elders for helping me to give my mother peace while assisting me with closing that chapter of my life.

At first, you had no idea that I flew my half of my mother's ashes home with me or what I'd planned to do. I was not going to share any of that with you but when we spoke in person it came out unexpectedly. I finally laid her to rest. It took me 3 years to gain the strength. That was the purpose of me spending so much time in Barnwell. I had to take my mother back home.

When I arrived in Columbia, South Carolina I exhaled a deep sigh of relief. I'd finally made it home. Metaphorically, it felt like it'd taken two whole lifetimes to get there. It literally had, I was exhausted. The drive up to Columbia from Myrtle Beach took a little over 3 hours. I stopped as often as I could to give Bella fresh drinking water along with allowing her to relieve herself. She was indeed an angel.

That was the farthest distance that I've ever driven solo. Earlier that year, in February of 2019, I'd vacationed in Atlanta for Superbowl LIII. My Airbnb was in Jonesboro, Georgia while all of the festivities took place in downtown Atlanta. The round trip car rides each day tallied up to approximately the same amount of time but city driving versus back-road country driving pales in comparison. I surprised myself, I had no idea that I could do it. I guess that the saying is true after all, we can do anything if we tell our mind that we can.

I checked into our hotel, went for ice, then immediately showered and ordered room service. I fell asleep long before they arrived with my food. I needed to rest up, I knew that the next few days were going to be extremely busy with tons of driving and lots of energy exchanges. I had a ton on my mind.

That first day that I randomly stopped by your house was totally unplanned. I told you earlier that day I'd already contacted Aunt Sherry, letting her know that I was in town. She and I planned to meet up in Barnwell. I wanted to catch up with her while visiting you and my mother's school, Guinyard Butler. While there, we ran into the Mayor of Barnwell. We chatted it up with him and took photos.

Aunt Sherry and I caught up and shared good times.

Aunt Sherry hit the road ahead of me; she was driving down from Aiken. Since I was driving to Barnwell from Columbia, I figured that I had a tad bit of time to spare. I figured wrong. I was beginning to get anxious, knowing that I was in town to see you while you were none the wiser. At the last minute, I decided to just take a quick ride by your house. My intention was to re-familiarize myself with the old neighborhood. I wanted to see what feelings came up. I never intended to actually stop or to come inside that day but when I pulled up to your house, your cars were in the driveway and your front door was open.

Looking back on it now, I'm extremely thankful that our first meeting happened as it did. I told you then that I planned to come to your house on a day when there was nothing else on my "to-do-list." I told you then that my initial plan was to be fully prepared for confrontation. In my mind, I was totally ready to engage you with an equal amount of any rage that you may have tried to display toward me. Thankfully, none of that was necessary. When I walked up to your front door, I rang the doorbell, nostalgia hit.

We spent about thirty minutes talking. I told you that I had my dog Bella-Angel with me in the car. You told me that Bella was not welcome inside of your home. You told me that when I come back to see you on the next day, that I needed to leave her behind at the hotel. I realize now that I was not really welcome in your home either. I do not remember you even offering me a glass of water. I remember asking my father, "May I use your

restroom"? It was as if I was talking to a stranger in a public space. I know now that I was talking to a stranger. You acted as if you were

staring at a ghost, you were; I am my mother. I embody her spirit and her character. I have all of her best qualities and some of her flaws. I look just like her and I carry myself with her poise and power of presence. You pretended not to know who I was and I found it amusing.

Thankfully, I had a photo with me that I was sure you'd remember. I'd also packed my passport; something in my spirit told me that I may need it. It's weird that you wouldn't unlock your screen door until I went back to the car to grab those items and present them to you.

I Am Her;

You knew exactly who I was.
I do not care how much time has passed.
I look just like the woman that you grew up with.
I look just like the woman whom you knew everything about.
I look just like the woman whom you married and had two children with.
I look just like the woman with

whom you built a life; before you crashed the boat, Sir.
I am her.

You also have no idea that, prior to my trip, everything under the sun happened to deter me from coming home. I remember, at one point, my Aunt Lois finally broke down to ask me, "Why are you so hellbent and adamant about going home to see your father?" I remember very distinctly saying to her at the time, "I don't know why, but I have a strong feeling that it's something that I need to do, and it's time."

First, it was Hurricane Dorian; Myrtle Beach had gotten completely shut down. I had to start calling everyone down there to get first-hand news reports, as I checked up on the weather conditions. The beach hotel that I decided to book would not answer the telephone for almost two weeks straight; panic was starting to set in.

Then, Bella-Angel got incredibly sick. At first, I thought that she was simply experiencing a bad heat cycle. During my stillness, I had been spending more time at home which allowed me to observe and learn her behavior. She wasn't playful, she wasn't eating her food nor drinking her water; she slept all day long and cuddled under me all night. Her belly was swollen and she had a strange discharge. After two days of diapering, I took her to an animal hospital for an evaluation.

I learned that she'd developed Pyometra. It turns out that this condition is life threatening. She had to have an emergency surgery. I learned that Pyometra is an infection that can only be cleared up by removing her uterus. I also learned that most Pyometra infections are fatal if the poison leaks into her internal system and surgery isn't performed immediately.

The money that I spent on Bella's emergency surgery had to come out of my vacation budget. I did not have any reserves, so that set me back. Bella then needed medicine, two to three weeks of recovery time, new vaccinations and re-evaluation before being cleared to fly.

Had I not been at home in stillness to witness the changes in her behavior, she would have passed away. Had Bella passed away in 2019, I would never have come to see you.

What you do not know is that I'm an animal lover. I've already experienced the devastating trauma of losing a pet. Starting from childhood, we had to give away our two black Labs, Spunky and Spurt, once we were put out of our last childhood home on Dartmore Lane in South Carolina.

We piled up what little belongings we could into the car and drove up North, so that my mother could gain the support that she needed from her family in order to help raise us. We were forced to leave behind everything and everyone that had shaped and molded us. We moved into a three story, five-bedroom/two-bathroom home that we labeled "Grandma's house." It was Public Housing that was already filled to the brim with various family members, including aunts, cousins, and an uncle. I slept on the couch in the living room, my mother slept on a foldaway bed in the dining room while my brother shared a bedroom with my youngest uncle. There was no room for two Labrador Retrievers nor were pets even allowed in Public Housing.

Fast forward many years later, once I moved into a home of my own, I got a puppy. He was a pure breed Mini-Poodle. I named him Bently. He was not named after the car, hence the spelling. I got Bently at eight weeks old and trained him with ease. I never got Bently neutered because I felt like it was animal cruelty. One day I took Bently to get groomed. I trusted his Veterinarian with his grooming. I'd been taking Bently to the same Vet for well over ten years.

Bently's hair was severely matted but I liked to keep his hair full and curly. He did not enjoy me brushing out his hair knots, so I left them, fully trusting that he'd be in capable hands with his vet. I dropped him off early one Saturday morning, then I went on about the business of my weekend errands. I got a call about an hour later as I was driving. I looked at the caller ID on my car Bluetooth, which read the name of his Vet. I was confused because I knew that he could not have been fully groomed and ready to be picked up in that short amount of time.

As my brain was processing why the office would be calling me so quickly, I answered the telephone. I figured that maybe they just wanted to give me an update or to simply let me know that they would have to cut his hair shorter than we initially planned. What I heard next made my heart stop, my world stood still.

The office staff never asked me where I was, if I was in public or if I was sitting down. I was driving down Roosevelt Boulevard on my way to Target. I remember hearing the words "Your dog asphyxiated after we gave him anesthesia". I remember immediately being blinded by tears and almost running a red light at one of the busiest intersections in the city. I remember my body turning ice cold and numb. I remember pulling my car over to the side of the road. I just sat there staring at nothing. I think I started screaming into the telephone when they asked me if I wanted to see him or come back to pick up his clothes, his tags and his leash. I never went back.

I remember pulling off after a while to go to the car dealer. I had an appointment that same day to have my car serviced. I do not remember much else about that day aside from calling my Uncle Rodney. I sat at the car dealership screaming to him on the telephone. He was devastated over Bently's passing too.

Even as I write this, I do not know how I went on about my business on that day. I got Bently when he was eight weeks old and had him for over ten years. He was family. He was the smartest animal and very protective of me. There are countless stories that many can share regarding him. The one weird thing about him was that he did not warm up to people easily, but he and my mother had a special bond. She had a way with him that gave him a sense of peace and calmness.

Whenever my mother came over to my house, she would always sit in her favorite chair while Bently snuggled next to her. It was the most peculiar thing. He never did that with anyone else. Bently barked a lot; he suffered from separation anxiety because I often left him at home alone. He was used  to a quiet environment and he was crate trained. Whenever I hosted family functions, I would usually tuck him away. During those times, my house would be flooded with tons of family inside and out. Being around a lot of unfamiliar energy made him anxious, so he'd follow me around the house as if his life would be over, had I left his sight.

There were a few occasions where he'd gotten loose and ran outside chasing after me. Once he got outside without a leash, he was quick. Before I knew it, he had run two or three city blocks. I would scream "Bently!" Everyone would go running after him trying to catch him. My Uncle Rodney cried with me on the telephone when I told him what happened to Bently. He made the calls to the family. I can still hear his devastated voice saying "Kim, no way, no way".

Uncle Rodney taught me how to properly train dogs; he and I share the same passion of being animal lovers. He has had a variety of animals throughout the years; Iguanas, Birds and such, but small dogs are his specialty. He is our family's Cesar Millan, "The Dog Whisperer." Uncle Rodney has experienced the grief of having to put a couple of his puppies down through euthanization.

I have watched this tough man who is a hard worker, dedicated husband and father who smokes marijuana and is absolutely obsessed with the comedian Dave Chappelle, cry until his eyes were red and bloodshot over the loss of his dogs. I often hear people say that losing a pet is like losing a child. I don't have any children, my pets are my fur-babies, so I echo that sentiment. Our animals become our family. They provide a level of peace and comfort that is indescribable. His current dog and cat look almost identical to my Bella and my cat Bleu. He's stated how the pairs act similarly; it truly is ironic.

I remember you telling me a story of how you and Uncle Rodney got into some weird altercation, one that he started, at my brother's high school graduation in 1992. You told me that you almost pulled your gun on him, but you had to calm yourself down and walk away.

Considering the circumstances, you being in his city and my uncle also being a licensed gun owner, I think that was the wisest decision for you to have made. I asked him about that altercation, he said that he had no idea what you were talking about.

Uncle Rodney has been more to me as an uncle than you have ever been to me as a father, so how dare you ever speak a bad word about him to me. He got married only once and has been through the trenches with his wife, Veda, for many years. Veda is a bonus aunt, my family adores her. He is a great father to his son and they have an amazing relationship.

My uncle's favorite food is chicken wings. He buys special orders of wings for his dog. My uncle's favorite movie is "Half-Baked". His favorite television sketch comedy series is "The Chappelle Show". My Uncle Rodney was once a Chess Champion, winning many Chess Tournaments. I have no idea what your hobbies are, Sir. I don't know any of the aforementioned when it concerns you.

Neither of my uncles were perfect men, as no one is, but they were

both dedicated husbands. I only say were, because my Uncle Richard, the eldest of my Grandmother Sarah's eight children, passed away in 2017. He was singing in church, performing a solo. He literally dropped dead right at the podium in front of the entire congregation including his wife.

Neither of them had any children outside of their marriages. My Uncle Rodney has one adult son. My Uncle Richard has two adult daughters. He fathered a step-daughter from his first marriage, as his own. Tyoni wasn't treated as a "step", she was his daughter. To this day, Tyoni is my cousin. Tyoni's one adult son, Anii and I share the same birthday.

Uncle Richard is truly missed. My uncles were best friends to each

other, until the day that Uncle Richard passed away. How dare you speak ill of my family, Sir.

Audacity;
How dare you have anything at all to say about my mother's parenting or our rearing when you weren't even there, Sir.
You made zero meaningful contributions to any phases of our lives.
We have been raised by a huge, loving family with lots of support.
You weren't there.
We lived in an environment that we were not of.
You weren't there.
We were sheltered and covered.
How dare you.

We had strong hands over us to show us what really mattered in life. That core foundation has never left us. We never got caught up in the hype of a superficial world. We never ran the streets, we weren't allowed to. We have been grounded in spirituality, love, kindness, fairness and humility. I despise the fact that you often have a negative connotation in your tone when you speak about my family. Ironically, you express that very

same sentiment when speaking about your own blood. Could it perhaps be YOU that you just do not like, Sir? You don't like yourself very much, do you. That's not a question, it shows.

On my journey, I've learned that people who rarely have anything kind to say about others usually behave this way simply because they don't like what they see in the mirror. They know that they are inadequate but they mask it by talking down on others versus admitting their own flaws. It's ok to say that you were wrong. It's ok to say that you messed up. It's ok to say that you don't know. It's not acceptable to me for you to cast judgement. You have no grounds, why would your mind tell that you did?

None of us are experts at 100% of anything. In fact, my personal opinion is that anyone who claims to be an expert is more than likely a fraud. We all make mistakes. Perfection is a myth.

What Self Love Looks Like;
Allow yourself; grace.
I've learned that the only way to show true strength is to admit your weaknesses.
Allow yourself; patience.
The only way to truly love yourself is to accept all of your flaws.
Allow yourself; time
In order to truly love yourself, you cannot hate any of the experiences that shaped you.

Chapter iii – Goliath
The Beautifully Tumultuous Pandemic of 2020

This part of my letter was the most difficult to write.
I know what I want to say, I just do not know how to say it to you.
I love you. I'll start there. I want you to know that, above all else.
There are words that you're about to read that you're not going to like, so forgive me.

It's a tough thing to force yourself to operate outwardly with tough love and strict boundaries when inwardly you are afflicted with the disease to please.

Once you read through to the end, I'm hopeful that you'll understand. If we never speak again and you go to your grave without ever feeling the need to properly respond, I'll be ok with that. My life will go on; I've always moved forward. My fear is the wake of destruction that your total legacy will leave behind.

March 1st, 2020, my Father called to wish me a Happy Birthday;
When you called me that morning I'd almost forgotten for a split second that it was actually my birthday. As I've gotten older the meaning of each one of my birthdays far supersedes any superficial level of understanding that anyone else could ever innerstand as I do.

Birthday Mood;

I was deep in a zone and feeling amazing.
I had the music on blast in the house.
I was singing and dancing as I was getting dressed for Church.
I caught a vibe and I was feeling good.
It was perfect that my Birthday fell on a Sunday this year.
I was listening to Kanye West's album; "Jesus is King".
I was looking forward to attending worship service.
It was a whole Birthday Mood.

I'd decided to really lean into my Mustard Seed Faith. It's the type of faith that is so tiny it's almost non-existent. The type of faith that can easily slip from your grasp if you look to the left or to the right of it. The type of faith that's almost an oxymoron. The type of faith that is so tiny yet so enormous because when you lean solely on it, believe in it, looking straight ahead at only it, feet firmly planted in it, God works miracles in your life.

My ringer is always off but I see every notification, so when I saw you calling, I stopped in my tracks as my hands started to shake. My palms were sweaty and all of my thoughts left me. In one swift movement, I put down my mascara, paused the music and walked out of my bathroom. Grabbing my telephone, I sat down on my bed, wrinkling my dress. When I answered my telephone, my voice cracked. I had allowed all rational reasoning to abandon me. As an adult, for the very first time, my Father was calling to tell me Happy Birthday.

Inner Wounds;

Again, the 4-year old Daddy's girl showed up; your baby girl, Ken.

The little girl inside who never knew as a mature woman that I'd longed for nothing more than to hear your voice every March 1st.

The little girl who loved you so much that I still remember that last day in our garage, way back when, the day that you left.

I was the little girl who remembered every moment from that last day.

The little girl who still remembers how you bent down to meet me at eye level placing me on your knee; you had some strong knees back then.

You said to me "Ken, I have to go now but I want you to know that I love you.

Your mother and I have to separate, she asked me to move out".

That Trauma birthed a child with fears of rejection.

That Trauma birthed a child with abandonment issues.

That Trauma birthed an inner wounded child.

I did not understand what any of that meant at the time but the one thing I understood was the look in your eyes and the sound of your voice. I still don't know what your last words were to my brother on that day. I still remember today how much pain you were in way back then. I know now that today; you are still holding onto that pain.

On March 1st, 2020, I was overwhelmed by your telephone call. I remember getting to Church and immediately telling Shalaya all about it. I was beaming with pride.

I forgive you immediately, over and over and over again. Looking back now, I feel like an idiot. It was as if I had forgotten that you let me down just three short months prior. Again, I was Daddy's girl and you were my protector.

You asked me what I had planned for the day. I told you that I was walking out of the door for worship service. I also told you that I had a few other things going on but my excitement about my plans to go Skydiving slipped out.

You told me how crazy of an idea that was and quickly reminded me that you have no idea how all of these outlandish adventures, love of animals and ways of being were engrained in me. I now understand why it doesn't make any sense to you, you don't know me at all.

You and I laughed on the telephone and we cracked jokes. You told me to be safe and I hung up feeling like I had just hit the Jackpot at the Casino after playing for hours or that I had just hit the Mega-Millions Lottery after playing the same number for 39 years. I was on Cloud 9. So high in the clouds that I ended up being 30 minutes late for Church. As I think about it now, it's partly embarrassing and as I come back to myself and the realization of what's true about me, I'm totally embarrassed to have spoken so highly of you to others.

What Embarrassment Looks Like;
*I'm embarrassed that I let you let me down.
I'm embarrassed that I've ever handed my power over to any other damaged soul.
I'm embarrassed as I look over all of the adversity that I've overcome.
All of the demons and dark spirits that I've battled.
All of the depression, anxiety, pain, struggle, stress, heartbreak, disappointments, lack, self-doubt, ridicule, bullying, the projection, the judgement, the misunderstandings, the arguments, the false narratives, and the two childhoods and decades of trauma that I have survived without you.
I'm embarrassed that I ever put my self-*

worth in the hands of anyone who is insistent on telling me who I am not when I know exactly who I am and whose I am. I'm embarrassed for others that I have allowed to have the audacity to project their fears and insecurities onto me not knowing, that one indicator alone and lack of empathy is a clear sign that they don't know who they actually are.
I'm embarrassed as I'm strongly reminded that I've endured and overcome all of that without you, yet I still felt that somehow something was missing because you were not an active part of my life.

What Forgiveness Looks Like;

I love you.
I am beyond unnerved with myself that I let my guard down without you proving your words with action.
I love you despite your flaws.
I am disappointed in my unrealistic expectations of who you are as a person.
I love you despite yourself.
I am disappointed in my unrealistic expectations of who you are as a Father.
I still love you.
I love you because you are my Father.
I love you because you loved my Mother.
I love you because you were always where I needed you to be.
I love you because you helped to create me.

Disconnected;

You were always one telephone call away.
You were always one plane ride away.
You were always one handwritten letter away.

I'm more willing to forgive you than you are to forgive yourself, because of that you're still stuck in the same cycle of behavior. Your behavior has cost the lives of two of your grandsons whom you've never met. They were both taken from here due to gun violence.

When I speak to you about it, it's troublesome to me that you seem to take it with a grain of salt.

I still don't blame you for it. I blame your trauma, your Father Albert's trauma and your Mother Rosalie's trauma. It just so happens that you are the only living elder in this equation, so the buck stops with you, Sir. You are the last man standing. Once you know better, you do better. Why do you continue to choose excuses? Either you don't know any better or you chose to not do the work required to actually be better. No one is asking you for perfection; your responsibility as a father is to make real actionable effort to be present in our lives. You have six children by three women but as I understand it you're not active in any of our lives, with any consistency.

Wounded Children;

You and my mother were both two wounded kids when you met and fell in love in grade school.
Neither of you were emotionally mature, healthy or whole when you asked her to marry you.
You both graduated from the same High School then later broke up.
You don't know this but I know what happened to my mother during her senior year of High School.
I know why she never showed up on graduation day.
I know why she didn't walk across the stage to receive her diploma.
I know why Mrs. Geraldine accepted it on her behalf and later personally delivered it to her.
Mrs. Geraldine, her best friend, told me the entire story.
It floored me, taking my breath away.
How could you leave her to deal with that alone?
Were you the father?
Did she name him?

Did you see him before he passed away?
Were you too wounded to provide the emotional support
that was required of you?

As far as I know, my mother has never spoken about that to anyone other than Mrs. Geraldine; quite obviously her husband, Mr. Marvin knows as well. All four of you were best friends back then, did anyone else know? I do not think that any of my mother's siblings knew. I told my brother about it but I don't think that he was able to properly process that information. I could not believe what I was hearing when Mrs. Geraldine told me. There are countless stories that my family has shared over the years during our various family gatherings. Of course, there is a fair share of secrets, inner circle nuances that not everyone needs to know; however, I felt like I knew all about my roots on both sides of my family, especially the things that are the most significant and life altering but this story is one that I never knew.

Mrs. Geraldine waited two years after my mother's passing to tell me the story. In 2018, she and I were having a random telephone conversation one day, she seemingly just felt compelled. She made it clear to me that had my mother not passed away; she would've never uttered a single word about it. I understood and I respected her for that. That is what a best friend is.

I share with my mother a similar story from my Sophomore year of High School that completely changed the trajectory of my life, placing me on a different path. That was why I fell behind in my studies; almost got kicked out of school, having to pivot in order to graduate High School on time. My mother made it clear to me that I would not embarrass her by being kicked out of the top High School in the City. I had to test in order to be accepted and I tested off the charts. She also made it clear that if I couldn't cut it by figuring out how to graduate on time, that I better voluntarily withdraw to figure out an alternate route, so I did just that.

I attended Central High School through 11th grade. I worked in the afternoons, then went to night school in the evenings. After completion, I withdrew, finishing out my Senior year by enrolling in Olney High School's Annex Program. It was a program designed to introduce High School senior's to Corporate America. The program was located off campus at the Naval Depot in Philadelphia. I didn't know anyone there. I had no circle of friends. I attended school for two hours per day, I then worked for four hours per day. The studies were remedial. I got straight A's every reporting period. I worked in the Naval Office's Human Resources Department. I was introduced to the corporate office structured environment of professionalism, militant discipline and military time. Those same lessons were put to great use later on in life.

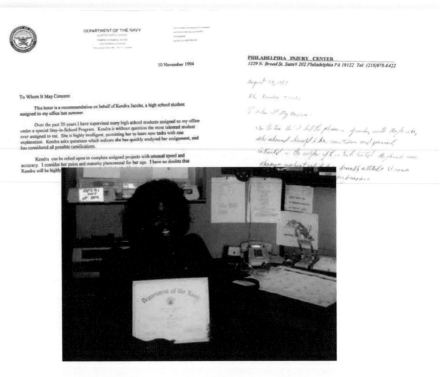

I remained an introverted loner while excelling at my job. I received high accolades and many letters of accommodation. It's amazing the suitcases full of pain that the women in my family have housed, yet we've always found a way to pick up the broken pieces of our lives to keep pushing ahead.

After High School, you went off to the Military, she moved up North with her family. You later left the Service and you came back for her. You convinced her to move back down South with you and she did.

The King's Family;
You knew that she was your soul mate but you hadn't matured enough to be the husband that she needed.

> *She loved you anyway.*
> *She saw her future in your eyes, so she said yes.*
> *She was so proud of her Family.*
> *She would often say that she had the King's Family and that she did it right.*
> *She told me that a King's Family marries, birth's a boy child first, then a girl.*
> *She had exactly that.*
> *You were her King.*

Now, here we are today, my mother is dead and gone, yet you have still never forgiven her for leaving you. It is as if you gave her a choice, Sir. She is my Grandmother Sarah, that is why you married her. She is my Grandmother Sarah, that is why she left you.

Choosy Lover;
She gave you a choice.
She endured your infidelity for years while trying to keep her family unit together.
She asked you to be the husband and family man that she knew you could be.
She asked you to stand up and give her the respect that she deserved but you just could not do it.
You chose to love my mother the way that you saw fit.
You chose deception.
You chose yourself.

She knew that you were having an affair with Jenny. She'd found the love letters. How ironic is it that decades later Jenny retired from her career at Bell South while I worked for the same exact Company, later resigning from my career after 19 ½ years at the Northern District of what began as Bell Atlantic?

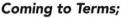

Coming to Terms;
Don't you realize that my mother had to leave you?
Don't you know that our steps are ordered?
Don't you know that you would have completely ruined her if she had stayed?

We struggled a lot at first after we moved up North; my mother was bred as a housewife who took great care of her home and her children just as my Grandmother Sarah modeled. After your divorce, she had to figure life out, but boy did she figure it out. You don't know any of this but my mother made a name for herself up here, just as her Father, "Man Simon", did down there.

My mother was "The Avon Lady". She created the most ingenious way to take care of us by selling Avon cosmetics as a Street Vendor. My mother sold hundreds of thousands of dollars in Avon merchandise. She won countless top seller awards and was placed 1st in her district over and over and over again. She recruited my brother and I as her helpers.

At first, we were embarrassed to be working on a vending table. Although Street Vending was a huge culture up North, we hated walking from school everyday to go down the street to work with her at her Street Vending Station while our friends went to after school activities or were hanging out just having fun. As I look back now, that was another life lesson that she instilled in us early on simply by actions not words. She was showing us what was important in life and that sheltered us from some of life's ills.

After a while the word was out, the money was rolling in and we were on board for the fruits as well as the labor. Eventually, most of our family came on as helpers too; aunts, cousins and all. The entire front room of our home used to be filled from floor to ceiling with boxes of Avon products. The boxes would block our walkway and we would always be embarrassed to invite our friends over. The UPS delivery man would pull up to our house and just shake his head as he unloaded box after box into our tiny home.

She sold all of the staples like; Skin-So-Soft, bubble baths, lotions and liquid deodorant. She sold all of the popular scents for women like Topaz, Timeless, Sweet Honesty and Imari; there were also products for men like Black Suede, Wild Country and Soap on a Rope. We would tote crates and boxes of smell goods to and from the trunk of her car to the streets of historic Germantown in Philadelphia.

Her stationary spot was on busy Chelten Avenue right in front of the Telephone Company. At that time Bell Atlantic was a monopoly in the Telecom Industry. Her stationary spot had high visibility with lots of foot traffic. She had brilliant foresight; she knew that the ladies working in the satellite office of the bill payment center would be eager to stop by her table to buy up the cosmetics. She knew that the customers going inside to pay their telephone bills would follow suit. She knew that she would gain repeat customers once the word got out that there was a woman who was selling the ever popular Avon products readily available on hand. You did not have to thumb through the booklet, place an order, then wait two weeks for your smell goods. You could walk right up to her table and grab anything that you wanted. She predicted lots of impulse purchases just like the candy, gum and magazines in every store, strategically placed at every front register while you're waiting in line to check out.

My mother knew that she would eventually scale her business by having order booklets in each customer bag, penned with her name and telephone number on them. She had small token samples that she used as free giveaways. Her business grew so big that she eventually started order deliveries by car. She then had to expand to a second vending table. She scouted out a small strip mall called Progress Plaza. The strip mall was in North Philadelphia, close to where we grew up, directly across the street from the Freedom Theatre and the YMCA, where she chose a spot right in front of the Payless Shoe Store. The plaza had a Super Fresh Grocery Store; a small black owned bank, then known as United Bank, a Popeyes Fried Chicken and a dry cleaners. My brother and I were tasked to manage the second location after school and on weekends. My aunts and cousins were also major contributors. My mother would later rotate, often attending local flea markets or county fairs. All of our family members, their friends, her friends and our friends bought Avon products from my mother. "The Avon Lady from Chelten Avenue" was her tag name and she wore it with pride.

She then added the staple classic chocolate candies called Katydids (Turtles) to her inventory. She placed them prominently on the front corner of her vending table to grab attention. That one chess move brought in sales from otherwise uninterested passersby. She taught me how to tell if a customer intended to make a purchase or not and how to negotiate the close on a sale. She taught me who had ill motives and who simply wanted to waste her time. She showed me who planned to try to steal from her by gathering as a crowd, attempting to distract her then snatching a product off of her table and walking away.

She never did mind the little things. As I have matured, neither do I. We would laugh about it later as we counted inventory at the end of the day. We would play it back in our minds and figure out who stole what. We always chalked it up as their own karma that they would later answer  for. The most valuable lesson that she taught me, which still rings true today, is empathy. Some customers truly wanted to make a purchase; they simply did not have enough money. I would watch her be kind enough to give some items away for free. There would be mothers with daughters who did not have any money. She would gift the little girls a lip balm or some hand lotion then tell them to put their goodies in their purse. She truly enjoyed seeing others smile.

 Some passersby saw the gentle soul that she was and just needed someone to talk to. For those people, she allowed much grace. She would engage in great conversation, sending everyone off feeling good.

My mother did so well over the years that she won an all expenses paid trip to Hawaii along with countless bonuses and accolades. She kept her customers coming back by giving them deep discounts, eventually giving them the ability to pay with either a post dated check or a credit card. As an Avon Representative ordering in huge bulk volume, she received a 50 percent discount. That enabled her ability to allow the price haggling.

However, the secret sauce was her. She was genuine and she catered to the needs of her customers. She made gift buying and holiday shopping easier by crafting gift baskets from clear cellophane wrap and ribbon from the dollar store. She was resourceful, she was a genius.

My mother was the glue to the fabric of our family. The party did not start until she arrived with the camera. She took tons and tons of pictures. I have half and my brother has the other half. She organized family reunions and our family summer trip every year to Brandywine Picnic Park.

Our family color was red. Everyone wore a red shirt and we all piled up in cars as we caravanned to gather for music, amusement park rides, lots of food, laughter and love.

We always had family events. We gathered for everyone's birthday, not just milestone birthdays, I mean every single family member's birthday. There was always a family party. We gathered every Easter, we had a special Annual Mother's Day Brunch. We barbecued in the summer for the Fourth of July, afterwards we'd walk down to the Benjamin Franklin Parkway to see the fireworks show.

During summer barbecues, we had the traditional parties with all of the elders inside. As we got older, we had the after party with cocktails, etcetera outside. We gathered for house warming parties, card parties or simply for spontaneous get togethers for no special reason at all.

My mother loved to play cards. She taught me how to play Pitty Pat, Tunk and 2500. As I've gotten older I've developed a personal passion for playing Spades. We gathered for a feast every Thanksgiving, we had a family Pollyanna every Christmas. We gathered for New Year's Eve then went to Church at around 10pm to bring in our new year in service to God. We stayed afterwards for New Year's Day Sunrise Service including a buffet breakfast filled with southern staples such as grits and homemade biscuits.

My mother raised us in Church. We went to Children's Church, Sunday School and Bible Study. We were not allowed to celebrate Halloween as children, so we would gather at Church for Harvest Fest in October. The Church hosted this event every year, specifically for children to gather for activities. We were given lots of candy so that we would not feel left out when our friends went trick or treating, coming back home with baskets that were overflowing.

As I got older and moved out on my own, I deliberately rebelled by celebrating Halloween. At first, I would just decorate my house then dress my dog up in costume, while sitting on my front porch giving out candy.

Eventually I graduated to wearing full costume, makeup and all while attending Halloween parties with friends. One year, I actually won the best dressed award.

My mother instilled drive and excellence in us. I never feel satisfaction unless I am the best at what I am committed to.

My mother put me in Piano Lessons. We spent summers at Vacation Bible School or Camp William Penn. She always had us in some activity of sorts, we also traveled a lot. We were always on an airplane flying somewhere. Throughout the years, we took plenty of road trips. Every time we piled up in the car to drive to South Carolina, we'd stop off at South of the Border for souvenirs and fun. My mother took me on a cruise one year with my Grandmother Sarah right by our side.

I think that you know that we had two completely different childhoods. She put us on an airplane as kids, with a guide long before we moved up North permanently from South Carolina. Once school let out for the summer, she flew us up North to spend time with our family. We got a taste very early on of what life looked like from a completely different lens than what we were used to seeing. In Philadelphia, we lived in neighborhoods with crime and violence. That view was contrary to anything that we'd ever experienced in the South.

We were not allowed to curse in our home. My mother did not curse, drink or smoke and she did not allow anyone else to do it around us or in her presence. It took many years before I'd ever see my mother actually consume alcohol. Even then, it would only be on special occasions.

Our home was filled with music all of the time. On a Saturday, as we were cleaning, we turned the music up and completed our household chores while listening to a variety of artists. We listened to lots of praise and worship gospel music along with an equal amount of secular music.

We grew up on Bebe & Cece Winans, Yolanda Adams, The Isley Brothers, Al Green, Marvin Gaye, Sade, Stevie Wonder, the list goes on and on. As we grew older and developed our own personal tastes in music, she allowed us to listen to other artists as long as there was no vulgarity. Music has been my saving grace, the soundtracks of my life.

My mother put the fear of God in us through her stern hand. We were terrified of her. We knew to respect our elders. We knew to say sir, ma'am, please and thank you. She instilled discipline and responsibility in us early on. We had chores, and we were given an allowance. She placed books in my hands as a pre-teen. She and I shared an obsession for reading. She would allow me to read her steamy Danielle Steel romance novels. That's where my love of solitude began.

I would lock myself in my bedroom from day to night, just reading. She would allow me to stay up all night long to finish a book. My eyes bled as I'd turn page after page fully engrossed in the stories. She left me to my own devices as long as I got up the next day to make it to school on time. One year for Christmas, she gifted me with a diary and an ink pen. That's when my passion for writing was born. She encouraged me to use my own creativity in my writing. I had an equal amount of passion for the art of music. I fell in love with the honest vulnerability and introspective transparency displayed in song. I'd listen to a song on repeat getting lost in it.

She and I would introduce one another to some of our personal favorite tracks. She introduced me to "Got To Give It Up" by Marvin Gaye. She and I discussed the tragedy of his passing. I played that

song over and over so that I could decode the lyrics and the melodies. I'd blast the music, play, pause, fast forward and rewind a song again and again on our living room stereo. I'd stay up nights obsessed with writing out every lyric just to understand the words. Eventually, she bought me a pair of headphones and left me to my passion.

Finding your Purpose;
As I reflect, I now understand that this is who I always was.
The secret to discovering who you are always lies in who you were as a child.
The secret to your gifts, your God-given purpose lies in your daily routine.

She taught us how to cook a basic meal for ourselves and how to do our own laundry. We were responsible for cleaning up after our pets, keeping a tidy room, washing dishes and taking out the garbage. My brother and I were given gender roles, we split our chores accordingly. As teens, we were responsible for paying the bill for our shared teenage house telephone line and responsible for paying our own pager bills.

She gave us matching radio alarm clocks. She taught us to prepare our clothing for school on the night before. She would have us choose an outfit, iron it, then hang it up. She had us pick out our undergarments, laying everything out so that in the morning we weren't scrambling around, rushing to get ready for school. We'd each set our individual alarm clocks while her voice of rath played out in our minds. She told us; "You better get up on time and get to school on time, I don't want any teachers calling me to say anything about you". We fully complied.

We enjoyed great Christmases. She'd ask us both for a wish list, she would then buy us almost every gift on our list. She'd sneak them into the house one by one. She would sit for hours after we'd gone to bed, tediously wrapping every single item, then place them all under our Christmas tree.

My brother and I could never contain our excitement, so every year he and I would devise a plan. We would both sneak into our living room, as quiet as church mice, together at around 3am. We would tip-toe into the living room in only our socks so that we wouldn't make any noise. We would sit down together on the floor right by the Christmas tree, marveling over all of it.

We made a pact to choose just one gift a piece to strategically and ever so gently unwrap. We just wanted to peak inside to see what we had. She was amazing at gift wrapping. The wrapping paper would be folded and tucked in at the corners, the scotch tape would seal the paper like glue. We agreed to choose one gift a piece to peak at but they were varied in size, it was extremely difficult for us to pick just one present. We had to be sure not to rip the paper. We would then place the tape back exactly as it was, resealing the gift, putting it back under the Christmas tree. We'd go back to bed but we barely slept, our eager anticipation was met with excited insomnia.

The next morning, while music played and our mother took photos, we'd open every gift with pure glee while my brother and I secretly eyeballed each other, maintaining our unspoken pact once we each got to the gift that we'd already opened.
I miss those days.

My mother found true love again. Mr. Vince was amazing to her, my brother and I. They traveled the world together, enjoying each other immensely. She has been to several places that I have yet to visit. She's seen and has experienced plenty of the finer things in life.

Mr. Vince was Jamaican, they traveled often to his home in Kingston, Jamaica. She would task an aunt to come stay at the house with us, while they were off in love and loving life.

Mr. Vince's sister and adult daughter lived in Kingston, his family welcomed and loved my mother. Our family loved Mr. Vince equally as much. He fit easily into our family dynamic and family structure. We all loved his energy. My Uncle Rodney got along with him the best, sharing their love for herbal libations.

Mr. Vince was funny and had a hearty laugh. I fully understood why she fell in love with him. He had a warm and welcoming personality. He adored, respected and protected her. He was patient with her and he had wisdom. He taught her a multitude of new things. He never tried to make her feel less than for not knowing what he knew.

My mother was a Heterosexual-Sapiosexual, as am I.

The first time that I ever traveled to Jamaica was with them. I spent almost two weeks in Jamaica with them during that trip. We flew into Kingston where we stayed for a few days; we then traveled to Ocho Rios for a few days, ending our trip in Montego Bay.

We climbed Dunns River falls together, went to clubs and dinners together, sharing great food, fun and laughter. That trip to Jamaica was the first time that I had ever ridden on the back of a motorcycle. It was the first time that I drank Red Stripe beer. I danced in gritty underground Jamaican nightclubs. They also allowed me to venture out while exploring on my own. The locals called Vince "Mr. Fudgy". He got that nickname because he was born and raised in Kingston, one of his first jobs was selling ice cream, from a Street Vending Cart, to the locals.

Mr. Vince was my co-signer on my very first brand new car that I purchased. I was in my early 20's without much established credit. I told my mother that I needed a co-signer, Mr. Vince was "Johnny on the spot" with no questions or hesitation. He drove me to the car dealership, helping me through navigating my purchase. My mother was not present that day because she was working. She knew that she left me in capable hands. He and I had a strong bond; a daughter/father-figure relationship outside of my mother. She set the standard that her children would be treated well by any partner who came into her life.

Mr. Vince paved the way for me from that point forward when it came to new car purchases. I did well with maintaining timely car payments. I eventually upgraded a few years later to purchase another new car, then another one. After I paid my third new car completely off, satisfying my loan financing contract, I decided that I wanted to be free of car payments for a little while. I settled into that vehicle for a few months. I'd maintained the car maintenance and it still had plenty of warranty left on it. I purchased a new car radio and had it detailed inside and out once every couple of months. My car drove smoothly, giving me no issues at all. I really only drove it back and forth to work or locally within the city limits, so the mileage was extremely low for an almost 5-year-old car.

Winters up North are pretty brutal with the heavy snowfalls and the ice storms as well as the pot holes in the streets so the tires on that car were starting to get balled. As a birthday gift one year, my mother paid for me to get four brand new tires, I was content.

Then the itch started after about 9 months. I wanted something new. I remember spending a significant amount of time online researching a very specific foreign car that I loved. I learned that it was best to purchase a certified pre-owned foreign car. A friend of mine, at the time, was living with me. She found herself in a tough spot, I had a three bedroom, two bathroom house with a fully finished basement to myself, so I loaned my couch and my spare bedroom to her and her two children in need. I was not charging her any rent.

I was apprehensive about pushing the button on purchasing a new car even though I'd spent a significant amount of time in my home office on my computer daily obsessing over this car. One day she said to me, "Let's just drive over to New Jersey to the car dealership and see what they have to say". I will never forget that.

My credit was excellent back then, my car payment history was stellar, so I said; "Ok, come on let's go". I had my signed car title in my hand and drove my almost 5 year-old-car with low miles, brand new tires, a new radio and leftover warranty to the Jaguar dealership in Cherry Hill, New Jersey. I drove off of that car lot with Jaguar dealership financing, without putting a dime down. I had a car payment of less than $300. That was in the summer of 2008. I bought my dream car, a certified pre-owned 2005 Jaguar S-Type, champagne gold. It had a 6 disc cd changer in the trunk and an almost unnoticeable beautiful pinstripe detail on either side. I had the dealership customize my Jaguar with my initials italicized and etched in the paint on both the driver and the passenger side front doors. I had custom Gucci headrest and steering wheel covers sewn and installed to match. I purchased and registered with the state, a personalized license tag "GDS-G1FT" (God's Gift). I remember people assuming that my license tag meant that I thought that I was God's gift. It's a shame that even when I humbly tried to explain myself by saying "No, this car, my dream car, was God's gift to me", I wasn't believed.

My friend, at the time, and I spent what felt like an entire 8-hour workday at the car dealership, but I vividly remember the moment that they handed me my keys. I opened the moon roof, and I felt the sun on my shoulders. As we were driving off the car lot, the first cd that I popped in was the album "Graduation" by Kanye West. The first song that I played was "I Wonder". That song has so much meaning to me for so many reasons. We sang at the top of our lungs, and I hit the brakes to the beat of the song as we drove down Haddonfield Road back home across the bridge. It was as if my car was the beat and I was the artist. Had it not been for her encouraging me to take a leap of faith that day I probably would never have experienced that moment. It's moments like that that are monumental. Moments where someone else plants a seed, your mind waters it, then it grows.

That brief moment was happiness.
At the time I thought that was success.
Peace is constant.

I did not realize until about 1 year ago that I now live 20 minutes away from that same exact car dealership. I drive by there often as I wait patiently for the day that I'll purchase my next Jaguar. I have the image of my new ride already etched in my mind.

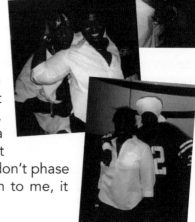

That is how manifestation works.
Life always comes full circle.
                    Duckworth.

Do you understand now that none of that would have happened if my mother remained married to you? I would never have had the courage to live life or have experienced any of those beautiful moments in life, had she stayed. I would never have experienced solo travel in foreign countries.

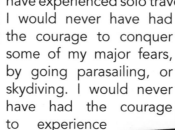

I would never have had the courage to conquer some of my major fears, by going parasailing, or skydiving. I would never have had the courage to experience f o r e i g n cultures, or foreign cuisine.

I have met some of the world's most famous people, walked right up to them, held a regular conversation and thought nothing of it. Those types of things don't phase me, fame seems more like a burden to me, it can be a drug.

I have pictures of some of those encounters, some of those moments I do not. Some memories remain so precious to me, so near and dear to my heart that asking for a photograph simply would've ruined the experience.

"Celebrities" are regular people, just like you and I, who experience the same human emotions, have the same human fears, and share the same human passions that everyone else has. Their bank accounts may be larger, their talents may be on display for the whole world to see, they may have acquired more life experience, or secured more assets but their desires for love, peace, and understanding are universal desires. We all simply want to live the most fulfilling, enriching life possible.

I have traveled alone to places where I do not speak the language, with a budget of less than $1,000. I have traveled for a week or more with almost no budget and I figured it out. I would not trade any of those experiences for anything here on earth. I have those stories, those memories, and those photos that live on in my heart forever. People may assume that it costs a lot to do that, but it doesn't. All you have to do is a little research and get creative.

I am still figuring life out, one day at a time. A smile, being kind, courteous, respectful, genuine, honest and generous translates in any culture. I have seen some of the most beautiful sunrises and sunsets. I have met great people by simply building human universal rapport. My mother and I shared a special bond with lots of love, laughter, arguments, and tears but that is life. It took her passing away and this reflection in order to realize that she was always my best friend.

I've had many friends throughout many phases in life, each one was always welcomed into our family. My brother and I share that same experience. His friends became my friends and vice versa. Our friends then became sons and daughters to our family.

Most people are building blocks and stepping stones that shape who you are becoming. Every person you encounter in life will teach you something about yourself. Some people simply teach you how not to be but all of it is essential to your growth. I would not trade those moments for anything in this world. I've learned so much about life as well as myself through those experiences.

Dear Mama;

Mom, you knew that I loved Tupac but I cannot take credit for the title of this prose, that was you and your son's song.
Mom, he played this song for you often, you made him a momma's boy, back then his emotions would soften, I understand why he couldn't say so long.
Mom, this was especially hard to write, through my wrongs, I realized that you were always right, I still cannot believe that you're gone.
Mom, did you know that I was always grateful when I was being hateful, especially when I wouldn't listen?
Mom, you raised us well even when we were going through hell, there was nothing missing.
Mom, we never went hungry, you were gracious, kind and funny you made all of our dark days

sunny.

Mom, do you remember my prom dress? It was gorgeous, black and gold and fully beaded, I had to have it, I was a bratty mess. You bought it without hesitation, you didn't care at all about the money.

Mom, I never sold my gown. We fought so much over the fact that I only wore it once. I still have it, one day I'll get it tailored to fit. I'll wear it, like a crown, as an honor to you.

Mom, we had many ups and downs despite all of that I still loved, cherished, adored and respected you through and through.

Mom, isn't this the order of things? Isn't the child supposed to bury their parent? Why was this so hard for me to accept?

Mom, it's because you're not here to witness my evolution, I'm in this new chaotic world caught up in this illusion, I don't know who to trust there's so much confusion. I don't know my next steps.

Mom, they will not tear nothing down, I won't let 'em. I built this home for you mama, you laid the foundation, I've just been working with so little time for personal. I know I promised you that I would make time for happiness.

Mom, I still love rap music, that last line was ripped from some of Drake's lyrics, I have to laugh to keep from crying, most days I'm a beautiful mess.

Mom, one of our favorite movies was "The Shawshank Redemption" I know every line of every scene. I've seen it far too many times to count.

Mom, the character "Andy" felt like a caged bird, I sometimes feel just like him, he needed his freedom, he was innocent, he just wanted to get out.

Mom I miss our movie nights, but honestly and truly I just

miss you.

Mom, my favorite line in that movie is when Morgan Freeman's character "Red" says "Get busy living or get busy dying" I know you're smiling down and praying over me so that's exactly what I decided to do.

I thought all these years that at any given moment, once I was ready, that I could come to you and build that same type of bond. I thought that you would welcome me with open arms, being equally as receptive and willing. Do you have any idea what I feel like now? Do you have any idea what it feels like to think that my own father wants nothing to do with me? I internalized that at first. Do you have any idea that your absence and rejection initially set the tone for my fear of abandonment?

Don't you understand that I am now an orphan? At 39 years young I became an orphan. I've tried to express that to you but it seems that you could not care less. My mother passed away 4 months shy of my 40th Birthday. She wasn't here to usher me into this new phase of life, that blow to me was detrimental. My mother and I spoke often about me turning 40. It was my "scary age". She wasn't here to witness it. My mother told me that on the day that she turned 40, she woke up and every bone in her body ached. The day that I turned 40, I woke up in the Dominican Republic, looked in the mirror and saw a tiny wrinkle in my forehead.

I laughed to myself.

Not only is my mother gone, so is my family dynamic. Everything that I knew to be true about my life is now over. My foundation was snatched from under me all at once. I had no choice in the matter. Try as I might, I have no way of fixing it. I came to you hoping to establish a connection then begin to build a new foundation, but I now accept the fact that you are simply incapable. It hurts like hell, but I release you, Sir. I have other mentors and I lean on God as my father to guide me in the right direction. You're not equipped and I forgive you for that.

You were emotionally abusive to all of us by being one foot in and one foot out. I remember the day that you stormed over to our home on Brenthaven Road with your pistol in tow, in a crazy rage. My mother briefly re-married, his name was Mr. Godwin. Mr. Godwin was living with us in what you called, "Your home".

You guys had already divorced, but you were livid because she'd re-married and moved on. I can vividly picture the story of that day. When you arrived at our home you were cussing and fussing with your gun locked and loaded. Mr. Godwin came out of the house with his huge machete sword ready to slice your head off. My mother then went running outside, jumping in-between the two of you, stopping the fight, or any subsequent destruction. Why in the world would you choose to behave that way knowing that your babies were inside of that home? You were already gone, had things escalated, we could've also lost our mother.

How could you allow your rage to blind you into not caring?

I do not remember much else about that day, other than you eventually leaving. A short time later, Mr. Godwin got his green card and paperwork legalizing him as a United States Citizen. He then disappeared. My mother never spoke much more of him. I recently talked to Mrs. Geraldine about him. I wanted to find out what happened. She told me that Mr. Godwin wanted my mother to move to Africa with him, after they married but she refused. That was what set him off, causing him to leave, wanting nothing more to do

with her. The interesting part that I also learned was that Mr. Godwin bought my mother the home that we lived in, and eventually were put out of, on Dartmore Lane. Mrs. Geraldine told me that after my mother refused to do as he said, no longer in compliance with his demands, he also stopped paying the mortgage. Perhaps that's the reason why you've never been to that home. I have no way of verifying that story. I am ok with taking her word for it. Mrs. Geraldine has nothing to gain from making things up, she loved her best friend far too much, she has no reason to lie to me.

We had always heard the rumblings of a story of you having another daughter, older than my brother. Over the years, that story has gotten so diluted. The story that I believed to be true was that you were in the service stationed overseas. Before you two married, during one of your many break-ups, you'd fathered a daughter by a woman in an Asian country. We never knew any more or any less. We safely assumed that somewhere out there we had a half Asian, older sister that you had no communication with, whom we'd never meet. We knew that she was your firstborn child. To this day, we've still never met her.

Imagine growing up, believing that narrative, then finding out the truth on the day of your mother's memorial service. In November of 2016, I am walking into my Grandmother Sarah's house; after the repass and a long day of emotional rollercoasters. I am surrounded by hoards of people and food. All I wanted to do was crawl into a dark hole but I was starving. As I sit down to eat, my telephone rings. It's a South Carolina exchange on my caller id. I assume that it's one of my cousins, on your side of my family, whose telephone number I haven't programmed in, calling to offer their condolences. I answered my telephone, and there is a black girl with a southern accent on the other end of my line. As she proceeds to tell me who she is, while expressing her condolences, I felt like I was doing the mannequin challenge all by myself.

The room is buzzing; people are everywhere. Food and drinks are flowing. There is both laughter and tears, while I am stunned silent holding my telephone. I was in shock, completely caught off guard. I do not remember exactly what I said to her. I do remember rushing her off of the telephone by telling her that I would lock her number in and call her back later. It took three years for me to reach out to her again. I still cannot get my sister on the telephone. If I was her, I guess, maybe I wouldn't want to talk to me either.

I am still processing that trauma.

The same way that I sat in a hospice room with my nephew while he watched his grandmother transition. I held my mother's hand, and I talked to her until her body went from warm to ice cold. I sat there for hours. It felt like years. I do not know how I was able to make the telephone calls to my family. Maybe I didn't, maybe Jr did. Maybe Jr was a lot stronger than I thought he was. I know now that Jr needed trauma counseling along with intense therapy after that experience.

I often wish that I had not picked him up that day. Jr had just gotten back home after being away for quite some time. He had not seen his grandmother yet in her last days; he hadn't had the experiences that his sister had. He hadn't spent the hours, days, weeks and months that she did with her grandmother, while she lay in the hospital for almost 6 months. As soon as my mother fell ill, I made sure that my niece and their mother had ample opportunity to spend time with my mother. My brother and their mother also met at very young ages and shared a romance full of ups and downs with many break-ups over the course of many years. She, too, was welcomed into our family, splitting briefly during his time away in the Air Force. They later came back together to co-parent two children. I had no idea that the day that I picked Jr up to go and see his grandmother would be the day that she transitioned.

I sometimes still blame myself for Jr no longer being here. I remember having brief conversations with his mother about me taking temporary custody of him, bringing him up to the Northeast to live with me, in a quieter environment, a working class neighborhood. We were starting to feel that if maybe he was in a different environment surrounded by a different element that perhaps his behaviors would change. I knew that getting in between the dysfunction between her and my brother would be a fight. I'd had my fair share of it over the years. I also knew that my freedom and my lifestyle would be taken away by being responsible for having a high-school-teenager under my roof. I shed tears often when I think of him and what could have been. I know that as more time passes the pain will ease away. Right now I dare to say, that's the one regret I have in life.

Jr;
My sweet nephew, I don't know where to begin.
I'm sorry and I love you now mean nothing, so why should I pretend.
You're gone forever, there are no take backs. I feel deep sorrow, hurt and pain.
I cannot imagine that what I feel even comes close to the emptiness that your mother and sister feel. I cannot quantify that rain.
I was there in the hospital on the day that you were born, your mother tried to give you the best life that she could but I think that you were cursed from that very day forward.
Sins of the father and his father and his father. But who's really to blame, do any of them feel ashamed?
Who should ultimately be held accountable for your scorn? The truth is that we all failed you. I'm equally as guilty too.

No, I was not your parent, I wasn't financially responsible for you but I could've done more to get you out of that environment.
You were just a baby, you'd barely turned 18, you were still wet behind the ears.
You were smart, funny and gifted. Jr you were heaven sent.
When I watched "Time", the Kalief Browder Documentary, I saw him in you.
Your sad eyes matched his, they said it all. I felt in my spirit that you would soon fall but I said nothing, I didn't want it to be true.
I feel that I'm a prophet and I know that I could've stopped it.

I felt it coming but I waited two years too late, I was hoping that grey skies would somehow turn blue.
Rana, my niece, you're still my Sweet Pea, no matter how old you get, this one's for you.
I'm sorry.

You never met my nephew, your grandson. Had you met him, I'm sure that you would have loved him as much as we all did. Jr was my brother's splitting image. Jr was handsome, charming, quirky, funny, gifted and talented. As a small kid he loved Elmo and I vividly remember days when the kids were young, I'd go pick them up to spend weekends with me, asking them what their music choice was before I popped in a cd for our car ride. The kids loved music as much as I did. My niece often introduced me to new art that I'd fall in love with. Jr would sit in the back seat of my car and would scream out "Play Beyonce!". I'd turn to playfully look at him asking him, "What do you know about Beyonce little boy?"

There is one specific Maxwell song that I still cannot listen to without thinking of him while becoming overwhelmed with emotion. The song is called "Pretty Wings". It was randomly playing on the radio, on one of our car rides. The car was silent that day, I guess all three of us were in our own thoughts. All of

sudden Jr starts singing along to the song, at the top of his lungs, in perfect falsetto. It's been a little over 1 year since his passing and I still don't quite know how to process that loss. I cannot imagine what my niece is experiencing. They were best friends. Her childhood memories live in him. There are countless stories, memories and secrets that only those two shared. She was his big sister and his protector. Jr was a son, a brother, a nephew, an uncle, a cousin, a boyfriend, a friend, an artist, and a creator but mostly just a lost kid trying to find his way.

I miss him terribly every single day.

I was in a daze that day, as that room filled with more and more family. The one thing that I do remember was calling my brother. I remember having to tell him over the telephone that our mother was gone. I remember that exact moment, his exact words and exactly how he processed that trauma in that moment. I never let go of her hand. I remember her hospice nurse being very gentle and telling me that the ears

are the last to go, that she could still hear me speaking to her. I spoke to her and I prayed over her for hours. I believe that all of her strength and every ounce of her power was transferred into me.

My strength defies logic.

The mere fact that I have endured all of that without you almost enrages me at the thought of how I could have given you so much power. In 3.9 seconds, I gave away everything true about me and handed it over to you. How could I have lost myself again along with my faith just because you were on the other end of my telephone on my birthday.

Don't you know that you are supposed to call your children on their one special day. Don't you realize that you don't get a special medal of honor or an award for doing what a father should be doing.

These aren't questions.

How could I have forgotten how you failed me 3 months prior in such a way that has been so detrimental and has caused such a domino effect of scorched earth. More tragedy, more internal upset, more generational curses, more self-destruction, more self-medication, more mental illness, more trauma. More.

If you'd been diligent about following through with my ask perhaps the tragedy in December of 2019 wouldn't have happened.

I drove to New York in January of 2020. I had finally gotten tickets to be an audience member of what used to be one of my favorite daytime talk shows, "The Wendy Williams Show". My teens were shaped by her voice on the local radio and I watched her career grow from the inception.

Fashion for me is also art, and I come alive any chance that I get to wear unconventional fashion and/or drive up to New York City to model it. I crafted the perfect outfit to wear to her show so that I could stand out from the crowd. I spent so much time in the mirror that day that I arrived in New York far too late to be seated for her show. Arrival time was 9 am, I got there at around 10 am. As I pulled up to the venue, there was a mob outside. The show staff was not allowing in any more guests, despite having a confirmed ticket. I spoke with show producers outside, trying to work my usual magic of not accepting no for an answer.

The woman producer was kind and gracious, but she simply could not accommodate me. However, she stated that she admired my efforts in my attire for the show. She said, "If you can drive over to Dr. Oz's studio I'll give you a name of who to ask for and you can sit in on a taping of his show." I did just that by leaving my car in the parking garage next to the Wendy Williams studio. I then scurried to flag down a cab, hopped in and proceeded to ride over to Dr. Oz's. I'd planned a full day of escape in one of my favorite cities and figured that I'd still make the most out of it.

It turned out that Dr. Oz was doing an all day taping, cut up into several different segments to be aired on multiple shows. I was seated front row; my outfit was a conversation starter so I built great rapport with several of his staff members. I spent about six hours in his studio that day, afterwards I explored New York City a little, doing some light shopping and stopping for a bite to eat before heading back home to New Jersey.

As I drove home, I remember pulling over at a rest stop just as I was entering New Jersey. My phone had been turned off all day so as to not be a distraction. When I turned it back on I saw the flood of missed calls and text messages. Reggie, Q, Aunt Lois, and Aunt Sherry were all trying to reach me. Panic set in; I feared the worst. I knew that someone was either seriously hurt or had passed away. They have never before all called me, on the same day, back to back like that within a span of a few hours. I feared that something had happened to you.

I called Reggie back first, he delivered the news. He told me that his father, your eldest brother, my Uncle Bubba, was found dead. I could not believe it. I had just seen him a few short months prior when I was in Barnwell, South Carolina visiting him. Yes, he was sick, but he was in good spirits, he was his usual firecracker self. We shared so many laughs on that day. My mind went back to the time that we spent with him. It was the same day that Aunt Sherry and I visited Guinyard Butler School.

We stopped by to see Uncle Bubba, then Reggie and Q randomly showed up. We stood in the yard, Bella-Angel in tow. We talked and laughed, swapping family stories. He was sitting in a mobile wheelchair. Bella kept trying to jump up in his lap to lick him. He told me to keep my dog away from him and to not let her poop in his front yard. We laughed about that. I guess I'm beginning to understand that having a cute little 10lb fur baby dressed up in frilly pink clothing doesn't fare well with deep south culture. You guys treat my Angel like she is just a rat in a cuter outfit. You all have no idea what joy and comfort, a loyal dog brings.

I was so grateful for those memories with Uncle Bubba.

I remember calling you at some point, to find out if you knew about Uncle Bubba's passing and to ask if you were going to attend his funeral. You initially told me no. When I heard that you changed your mind by actually showing up, you have no idea how proud of you I was. Aunt Lois and Aunt Sherry told me that you attended Uncle Bubba's funeral. Not only that, I was elated to know that my sister Delois was there and that was how you two reconnected; I was moved to tears. It seemed that your hardened heart was softening. It seemed that you were beginning to take head to the words I'd spoken to you.

You and I spoke about your severed relationship with your oldest brother. You told me what I already knew, that you are not close to any of your side of my family and that you and Uncle Bubba had a huge argument many years ago that you guys never patched up. I told you to make amends with him. I told you that no matter what, at the end of the day, he is still your brother. Your grievances with one another could have easily been set aside by just having an honest conversation. How do you feel now knowing that you can never have another conversation with him?

I told you that time waits for no man, that he was really sick, so you needed to call him or just drive down to go see him. But, your stubborn pride and ego were in total control.

Ego Death;
Your ego will always hurt you in the end.
Your ego forces your need to be right.
You need to kill your ego.
Your ego only exists to mask your insecurities.
Your ego will always steer you wrong.
Check your ego or you ego will check you.

You and I have also spoken at great length about my sister, Delois. I told you that I still had her telephone number from when she called me in 2016. I verified through Aunt Sherry, who I later learned is closest to her, that her number was still the same. I wanted to see her so badly while I was at home visiting, I called her, left messages and text her but she would not respond. I tried reaching out to her for months. I totally understand that maybe this time around she just isn't ready. I told you all of this. I've asked you countless times to have her call me. You continually said that you would, but I wonder now if any of that is the truth. Did you need to keep her all to yourself so that you could keep up with your façade?

As you and I spoke throughout the Pandemic of 2020, you would tell me all about the quality time that you were spending with her, while getting to know her. I was initially very proud of you.

A Daughter's Pride for her Father;
I was getting to know my sister through you.
I was proud of you.
You told me many things about her that I could never have known.
I was extremely proud of you.
You told me that she too had a very gentle, sweet personality and that you drove down to Barnwell, South Carolina, spending your entire birthday week with her, helping her with home improvements, painting and rehabbing her home.
I was so proud of you.

You told me a little bit about her mother; you told me that her mother passed away when she was extremely young. I think you said that my sister was around 4 years old when her mother passed. She doesn't realize that she and I are bonded by our 4-year-old trauma. I wonder if my mother ever knew her mother. You told me that at one point you considered taking custody of her, but the situation got complicated. You said that she wound up being raised by her grandmother. You told me that you walked her down the aisle when she got married, I never knew that, I don't think that any of us did. You reminded me of the story behind her tragic loss of her oldest son. I do not remember now exactly how I found out, but recently I learned that she also lost her son due to gun violence. I remember learning that she asked you to come to her son's funeral. You promised her that you would, but in true Charlie fashion, you never showed up. I remember being told that all she wanted from you was for you to just show up to show your support. I wonder what it would have been like to grow up with my older sister.

As you and I talked on countless days for countless hours over the telephone throughout the Covid-19 Pandemic of 2020, I was beginning to feel like maybe we could actually establish a healthy father-daughter relationship. I felt like we were doing the Pandemic together. We were partners on the East Coast. I'd give you first hand reports of how my city was faring while you did the same by telling me all about how the folks in South Carolina were handling the Pandemic.

I distinctly remember the day that the NBA got canceled. I remember telling you on that day they were going to shut the world down and you disagreed with me. Do you remember that day? I remember the days leading up to the very beginning of the quarantine. My city felt eerie. My stress level was so high that I resigned from my job via email, that was on March 5th. I was on the telephone with you while listening to KYW News Radio, driving from store to store buying up every roll of toilet paper, paper towels, bottles of bleach, cans of Lysol, gloves, and masks that I could get my hands on. I remember my nervous anxiety being in overdrive and having to force myself to be still and meditate. That's when I began talking to God and listening in silence.

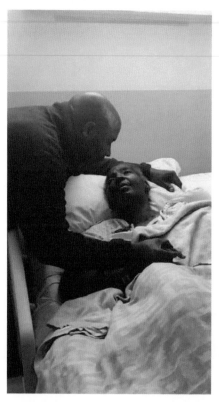

I remember us discussing having faith over fear while being cautious. I had high hopes of us making up for the many years of lost time. You would tell me often that you truly wanted to gather all six of your children together in one room to properly introduce us to one another. We'd rationalized together that Brian, Charlton, and Andrew would easily get on board. We talked out the plan together, concluding, now that you were playing an active role in Delois' life that she would also be eager. You knew that was all that I ever wanted. I just needed for you to say the time and the place, and I would be on a flight, Bella-Angel in tow. We rationalized that the wild card and the hard sell would be my brother.

A Son's Rage;

He is so angry with you, Sir.
He has every right to be.
I cannot imagine how he feels
as your firstborn son, born on
your birthday, with a family of his
own now, just trying to navigate
through life's ills.
A man whose father has always
neglected him and his children.
A man who lost his mother in
such a quick, detrimental way,
whom we were both so close
to, whom we leaned on as our
lifeline. Without any proper space
or outlet to shed his tears, bear
his scars or show his emotion
without a proper safe space or
covering.
I remember him reading the book
of Psalms to our mother while she
lay in the hospital for months,
unresponsive.
I remember her hearing her son's voice on that day and
waking up long enough to open her eyes and say his name.

I remember him breaking down into tears and me not knowing the right words to say to console him.
I remember allowing him grace through hugging him tightly.
I remember always feeling like his big sister in those moments.
I remember admiring my big brother's strength of vulnerability.

My mother had several strokes while she was in the hospital and she hadn't spoken for quite some time, but she heard his voice reading the Bible to her. She woke up that day and said his name. I cannot imagine how he feels having children of his own just trying to be the best broken and traumatized father that he was taught to be, to them. I cannot imagine how he feels, knowing that his father failed him. I venture to say that he fears that he has failed his own children. I cannot imagine how he feels knowing that his father is now a great grandfather who has never met most of his grandchildren nor his two great grandchildren and doesn't show that he has any interest whatsoever in taking any real actionable effort in meeting them, getting to know them or being an active part of their lives. That is the exact reason why I chose to never have any children of my own.

My mother tried to push me to have children on so many occasions. She and I started to have constant conversations about it whenever there was a disconnect within the dynamics of my brother and the mother of his children. She would tell me often that having a grandchild by her daughter would've been special to her and a completely different dynamic. In our family, the women are the ones who are the nurturers of their children. The women hold their children close.

My mother was also a proud grandmother. She loved and nurtured her grandchildren as if they were her own. She watched me nurture, love, and care for my niece and nephew from the time that they were born, as if they were my own. She watched how the men in my life, that I've dated, knew how much I loved and cared for my niece and nephew, how they treated them accordingly as extensions of me.

She watched as my niece and nephew would receive random gifts from an ex. Knowing that those gifts came as a surprise, even to me. I remember one year on my niece's birthday; she wanted a scooter. I had the kids at my house for the weekend as I would do often; my boyfriend, at the time, was also staying over. I planned to take the kids swimming, later we'd planned a little pizza party. All four of us got to the pool, my niece, nephew, and I immediately hopped in and started having fun. My boyfriend, at the time, told me that he had an emergency that just came up. He said that he needed to leave for a brief moment, but he was coming right back. I was confused. I knew that his children were fine and that his parents were fine. It was a Saturday, so there was no work emergency. I fully trusted him, so I quickly dismissed any suspicious thoughts. He left and came back about an hour later with a scooter for my niece. It was a surprise for her equally as much as it was a surprise to me. Yet even still I had the foresight to know that long term he would not have been a good candidate for me to have a child with. He was a good person and a good father to his own children, but he and I just weren't a good long term fit.

Unfortunately, most of the women in our family are single parents. I always knew that lifestyle wasn't one that I wanted to live. I honestly never had a strong desire to be a mother. Although my mother always wanted me to marry first, as did I, as I got older, she watched me move from one relationship to the next with ease. She began saying to me if I wanted children maybe I should just consider choosing the best candidate and taking a shot at it but that wasn't a smart move for me; that was her desire for my life.

I always had long term thinking. Back then I didn't have the language to properly articulate this sentiment but I knew from a very young age that at some point I needed to deal with my trauma. I always knew that if I chose to, I could figure out how to be the best parent possible and raise stellar children, with or without a husband or a life partner but that was never good enough for me. I knew that I was broken and I refused to birth broken children. As I look back today over all of the decisions that I've ever made in my life and all of the wrong turns that led me right to where I am today, I am grateful to

God that I stood firm in my decision.

While visiting you, we got to talking about your upcoming birthday. I asked you how old you were turning. I couldn't remember if you were one or two years older than my mother. You told me that you were turning 70 and you were extremely excited. Your facial expressions and your body language was totally energized. I got excited along with you. I asked what you were planning. This was a milestone birthday, you seemed to be in great spirits anticipating a huge party. You looked great, your skin was smooth, and you still have a full head of hair. Your weight was intact, so aside from that weird thing that you have going on with your teeth, you seemed to be in tip top shape. I asked you if Jenny and the boys were throwing you a party; you hesitated a little then said that you didn't know.

March 16th, 2020, your birthday.

After leaving South Carolina and flying back home in 2019, I immediately went to buy you a 70th birthday card that I never actually mailed to you. I called you first thing in the morning on March 16th to wish you a Happy Birthday. I also called my brother and I demanded that you call your son to wish him a Happy Birthday. As far as me giving you gifts; you haven't earned it, Sir.

Where were Jenny and the boys? Has she now left you too?
Why were you with my sister and not your wife, sons and their spouses

on such a huge milestone birthday. Do you really think that I don't notice and later analyze everything that you've said to me?

Father's Day 2020;
I had to fight myself to not call you.
I laid in bed and cried all day long.
I literally cried all day.
No television.
No social media.
No distractions.
I forced myself to feel my emotions.
I'm a grown woman.
It doesn't make any sense to feel this way about a father who was never there for me.
You don't deserve a "Happy Father's Day" from me.
You didn't earn a "Happy Father's Day" from me.
Does your mind tell you that you're a great father?

I wanted to call you so badly. I refused to give you that honor. All that I've ever wanted was to be able to call my father on Father's Day. You haven't earned those privileges, Sir.

After I flew home to see you last year, I remembered that one of the first questions that I asked you was about your health. I specifically asked you if you had any major health issues. I asked if you had been to the doctor for a complete examination. You have smoked cigarettes and you drink alcohol daily, almost your entire life. You said that your health was intact. You lied to me. I know that you are sick. I do not have any detailed explicit knowledge. I sense it in my spirit.

I think that you either have Prostate or Colon Cancer.

In late September, early October of 2020, I called you non-stop for about two or three weeks. I knew that something was off. For almost an entire year you and I have been in constant communication. As it always ends up after a while with you, it was mostly my initiation of communication. We'd found ourselves in sort of a rhythm where, if I called you and you didn't answer right away, I would leave you a message, then you would get back to me either the same day or the next. I remember calling you, then maybe 3 or 4 days had passed without a return call. I'd gotten busy with life stuff, as usual, so I set it aside, but I felt something. I called again, no answer, 2 days later, no return call. I called your cell phone, no answer. More days have passed, now I'm alarmed.

We're in a Pandemic of epic proportions. In our lifetime, none of us have experienced anything like this. Our entire world is in total chaos. I told you all about how triggered and disturbed I was behind George Floyd's murder and the aftermath of the subsequent riots. I told you all about my joint, organic venture in my local community to organize together to effect some sort of change. I told you all about the BLM Rally and peaceful March that we swiftly organized and executed on the Saturday after Juneteenth. I told you how we pounded the pavement together, registering people to vote and spreading the words of unity in our community. I told you how I was the only black woman on the team but I felt honored and proud that other races were just as concerned for positive changes in our little community.

Did it not occur to you that I thought that you were dead?

You've been telling me constantly that you've been outside here and there gathering household supplies and toiletries. I was beginning to fear the worst again. I thought for sure that you had contracted Covid-19 and that you'd either been hospitalized or that you'd passed away or that perhaps you'd gotten into a serious altercation during one of your store runs. Countless tragic events were taking place as I'm calling your house telephone and your cell from both my personal telephone number and my business telephone numbers. Eventually, I text messaged Jenny. I told her that I couldn't get you on the telephone and that I was worried. I asked her to please have you call me.

You obviously listen to her, which is a great thing, you got back to me immediately. I asked you what was wrong. You immediately said, "Oh nothing", you then made up some random excuse as to why you hadn't returned any of my calls. At first, I thought nothing of it. We continued on about our usual surface conversations. But something just did not sit well in my spirit. The tumultuous election happened, then the holidays rolled around. During this time, my emotional meter was off the charts. After that last telephone call with you, I decided to take a huge step back. I wanted to see if there would be any initiation to communicate with me, from you. That's when everything changed for me.

I also needed to re-center myself, that was my main priority. November 2020 was an extremely tough time for the entire world. I was way too dialed into all of the drama. I cannot function peacefully like that. Holidays also just aren't particularly my favorite time of year anymore either. I used to adore holiday shopping, decorating and gift giving. I'm now noticing that something internal triggers in me every year around this time. I started a tradition of escape through solo travel the first full year after my mother passed. In November of 2017, I flew to Costa Rica by myself just to spend 5 days doing absolutely nothing. That was blissfully peaceful. Because of the Pandemic I decided that it was best for me to remain at home and not do any traveling until it felt a little safer outside.

2020 didn't allow me to escape. I'm now grateful that I was forced to be still. I decided to work on my mental health by properly processing my grief.

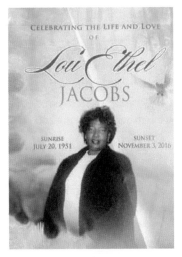

November 3, 2020 was Election Day. Ironically that's also the anniversary of my mother's passing. She and I had developed a tradition many years ago where every Thanksgiving Eve, she would come to my house and we would stay up all night long cooking and talking while preparing for the holiday. We would have great music playing, sometimes I'd manage to convince her to have a glass of wine with me. The next day we would go down to grandma's house to celebrate Thanksgiving with our entire family. December 11th is the anniversary of Jr's passing. This is the first full year after my nephew has been gone. I have been so busy working toward navigating my new life in a new state with a new career that I hadn't slowed down long enough to properly process or grieve my nephew.

Then I spoke to Aunt Lois and Aunt Sherry. They told me that you had been sick in the hospital during the time that I could not reach you. They told me that you went to the hospital in severe pain with bladder issues. They told me that the doctor had to place a catheter in you in order to relieve your urine. They told me that the hospital staff stated that you needed an immediate surgery. I heard that you then snapped out on them. They told me that you cursed out the doctors and stormed out of the hospital like George Jefferson with the catheter still inserted while leaving a cloud of smoke behind you.

Now I don't know if it happened in that exact way but from what I know of you and all of the stories that you have told me personally coupled with the stories that both sides of the family have told me about your temper, I would be willing to bet that most of that story is pretty accurate. I couldn't believe it. My intuition was right. My aunts also told me that at that same time, you stopped speaking to my sister because she told you that you needed to follow the doctor's orders.

I sat with that information, and I meditated on it. I meditated over everything that I just mentioned. I meditated over the entire beautifully tumultuous pandemic of 2020 and how the world has completely shifted. The world seemed to be off tilt to me at first but again I am realizing now that everything has happened exactly as it should have according to what has been written. This is Spiritual Warfare. You and I were both swept up in it.

I chose to get out of the way, stepping to the side of it. I chose to process this pain from an aerial view by applying the healthiest possible perspective. I do not choose to make it make sense. It already makes sense. Everything happens for a reason. When we are in the eye of the storm, sometimes we cannot see our way out of it, so you just have to ride the storm out. I was doing everything possible to try to force my own reality into this equation but one day it just hit me like a ton of bricks. I stood still enough to ride out the storm.

Do you remember the last telephone call that we had? I told you that there never seemed to be enough time and that it never seemed to be the right time to have a genuine conversation with you. I mean a deep retrospective dive into all of the things that we should be talking about, everything that I've written here. You seem to only ever want to carry on with surface conversations. I decided to put a stop to that. I told you on our last telephone call that I was going to sit down and write you a letter.

I do know, about myself, that I communicate much better when I can calmly organize my thoughts, while being completely still, writing them all out. That is the absolute best way for me to properly process and articulate my sentiments. Well, this is that letter, Sir. I decided to turn my pain into purpose. This is by far the most difficult project that I have ever worked on in my entire life. I could add so much more to this, but I have decided to pen this as an open letter and turn it into a book. This will be my first auto-biographical piece, and I am gifting it to the world.

Our world needs healing. There are so many broken children walking this earth in an adult disguise causing so much hurt and harm to themselves and others because we won't take the time to properly process our grief, grievances and traumas.

In obedience to the call on my life, I chose to share with the world what the application of healing my trauma through therapy, stillness, meditation, spirituality and applying a different perspective looks like. I had to decide what to do with my trauma if I wrote you this letter and you chose to ignore it by never responding. I'm ok with that outcome.

39 is now the world's guide to a healing journey. If my scars help just one person, I've done my work.

They said you're Depressed;
Are you depressed or are you unfulfilled with your lifestyle and your choices?
But they said you're depressed.
Are you depressed or are you overweight and underpaid?
But they know best, they said I'm depressed.
Are you depressed or are you sick and tired of being sick and tired?
I'm now so comfortable with vulnerability that it scares most people that I come across.
We are so used to hiding in boxes as if no one sees us.
We are tricked into thinking that our silence about our issues is protection.
Our silence is killing us.
Are you depressed or are you simply masking your trauma with substances?
Bottling up your emotions, while swallowing bottles of pills prescribed by some doctor who says that's the only cure is not the answer.
Hopelessness is not the answer.
A poor diet is not the answer.
Lack of exercise and dehydration is not the answer.
Are you waiting for someone else to come fix you or are you worth it to you to begin fixing yourself?
Are you depressed or do you binge watch trash television and inhale mindless entertainment?
Feeding your mind, body and spirit with normalized dysfunction is not the answer.

Lack of any proper channel or any outlet to let your
frustrations out causes internal disease.
Are you depressed or are you codependent, trauma-bonded
and soul tied to an unhealthy partner?
You will remain depressed because that's what you told
yourself.
You will remain depressed because that diagnosis makes
others wealthy.
You cannot heal what you refuse to look at.
You cannot heal what you refuse to change.
You cannot heal what you do not reveal.

As I look back over the year of 2020 as it concerns our pretty much false, non-existent relationship and the Covid-19 Pandemic, I am grateful for so many things. I have learned that you and I have spoken so many times yet we were always having a different conversation. You had your personal motives, I can now honestly say that I had my own as well. The difference is that my intentions and my motives have been pure. You have been hell bent on selling me whatever your mind told you that I would buy.

You finally decided to return my call in October. As my telephone vibrated, with you showing up on my caller id, I was a little irritated. I did not want to display my irritation in my tone so I remember playfully answering the telephone and saying "Who is this man"? You kidded back with me by saying "Well, you can just call me Dad, that'll do just fine". I have never called you "Dad". It is instinctual, I just never realized it until you pointed it out. I laughed it off with you, I still never said it. After we hung up that last time, I started to wonder if you even know the difference between what a dad is versus a father?

Jenny told me in November that you don't want her to communicate with me. She and I have exchanged many text messages throughout the tail end of 2019 and almost all of 2020 with our last one being a Happy Thanksgiving text exchange. I learned that she was sneaking behind your back to speak with me, text me and to share photos back and forth. Do you even care about how that makes me feel? I had no idea until she finally said it.

What is wrong with you? I forgave you and her without ever receiving

a proper acknowledgement for your affair that broke up our family, or an apology for the loss of my mother. I refuse to sneak around just to communicate with her behind your back. That's how you both started your affair and that's precisely why we are here today, with this outcome in all of our lives. I too have enabled adultery when I was young, immature and making dumb life decisions. Sneaking to speak with her behind your back is exactly what she did behind my mother's back. If I carry on with her like that, I will be dishonoring my mother's memory and her legacy. How dare you both, Sir
I refuse.

The Good in Goodbye;
I will never reach out to you again for any reason at any time about anything.
Thank you for turning my fear of abandonment into gracefully bowing out of situations that dishonor me.
Thank you for gifting me with my gift of finding the good in goodbye.
No matter how old I get, I turn into a child around you. I revert to being a 4-year-old searching for her father's approval. It isn't healthy for me and I cannot stand it. You act as if you are not the author of your legacy. Don't you care about what we will all have to say about you once you are gone? You are fully aware of your looming mortality more so than anyone else is. Why don't you want to try fixing it? Does your dash really not even matter to you? You act as if your creations are disposable and I will have absolutely nothing to do with any man who behaves in that manner toward his children, especially not my own father. It goes against everything that I believe in.

Hero no more;
You are my father
You saved my life once.
I thought that you were my hero.
Can you imagine my disappointment once I discovered who you really are?
You're no longer my hero.

You're a broken man child, a fallen star.
Dads are heroes.

I am tired of pretending with you. I do not have much else to say to you until you get help with facing yourself and your demons. You and you alone must decide to engage with the man in the mirror first, then all of your children in an honest, healthy way by fully owning your faults. You are flawed, as we all are. However, you make excuses for your mistakes. You blame others for them. That, Sir, is narcissistic personality disorder 101. That is a mental illness that can be passed down through your DNA.

I've held things back from you too; see what you don't know is that I recorded every sit down conversation that you and I have had with one another, while I was at home visiting with you. It's been over a year, I've never listened to any of those recordings until now. After everything that has happened, I could never bring myself to face the pain. My plan was to sit down with my brother, to play the recordings for him, after you'd followed through with what I asked of you. I envisioned he and I listening to the conversations, him having tons of questions that I could now answer, providing him with a healthier perspective and a way of viewing you that would allow him to get to a place of understanding and healing. I envisioned him and I having a good cry then talking and laughing like there was no tomorrow, the way that we used to many moons ago. I envisioned us reminiscing over the nostalgia of our childhood, while remembering how great it was, despite and in spite of.

There are things about me that only my mother knew, I wanted to be able to trust you enough to share them with you. There are major traumas that have happened to both my brother and I that my mother and some of our childhood friends have witnessed. I don't have the right to share a lot of it, especially not with you. I sat directly across from you looking you straight in your eyes, I begged you to call him. I told you how urgent it was. I told you that I was fine. I told you that there was nothing that I needed from you. I told you that my heart wasn't hardened toward you. I never hated or blamed you for anything, therefore, there was nothing for me to forgive. I poured my heart out to you. I told you that different children need different things from their parents. I told you that not all kids raised under the same roof will experience nor process the trauma of divorced parents in the same way. I told you how eerie it is that my brother has become you. He has repeated the exact same cycle that you set for him. He has caused the exact same traumas that you have caused.

Years before I flew home to see you, my brother landed on your doorstep in similar fashion. He never told me ahead of time that he planned to visit you but we spoke all about his trip and you afterwards. When he flew home to see you, you totally rejected him on the spot. I do not care what state he was in; he is your firstborn son. You abandoned him for a second time. How in the world could you not realize that additional layer of trauma that you added?

I now know why. You saw yourself and you couldn't face the mirror. Do you really not know that it isn't our job to hunt you down to try to force you to talk to us nor is it our responsibility to try to cultivate a relationship with you. You created us, we didn't ask to be birthed. You are still alive and breathing and I am sure that there are many life lessons that we can learn from you but you're still closed off and emotionally unavailable. That's a huge red flag and a clear indicatorof your traumas.

A small part of my visit home was selfish, overall I told you that I had a vision. I told you that I did not want to speak what I felt into existence because my words are powerful. I told you that I sensed something about to happen and if you could just wrangle your son, then he could wrangle his and maybe what I feared looming wouldn't actually happen. Maybe you could stop it in its tracks. I begged you repeatedly. Every time I came by your house and every time afterward when you and I spoke on the telephone, I made you promise me. While I was there at home, I spoke to Jenny privately a few times. She too, promised me that she would get you to follow through.

After my vacation was over and I flew back home, I continued to insist that you call your son and attempt to reconnect with him. I did not want to pressure you but I had to insist. My intuition is usually always right. During our initial telephone conversations you told me that you needed time to figure out what to say to him and how to approach the subject. You admitted to me then that you knew you were guilty and felt awkward calling him to give him parenting advice. I understood. I gave you a little grace. I was patient with you but I also was firm.

Imagine my disappointment when you finally nonchalantly told me that you called my brother, and he said he's doing just fine, everything is fine and you didn't sense the urgency nor did you feel the need to pry into his personal life.

He is you;
Did it ever occur to you that my brother is furious with you?
Did it ever occur to you that my brother is terrified of you?
Did it ever occur to you that my brother is holding onto anger and resentment because of you?
Did it ever occur to you that my brother thinks that he is a failure because of you?
Did it ever occur to you that my brother despised us having to move up North and feels that we have seen and experienced things that we should never have been exposed to and he blames you?
Did it ever occur to you that my brother enlisted in the Air Force because of you?
Did it ever occur to you that my brother hates you?
Did it ever occur to you that my brother is you?

All your son ever wanted, was for you to be proud of him. Can't you see that your firstborn son has placed his feet in the footprints left to him?

Dreams;
Yes, a large part of the reason that I flew home was to cultivate my own personal relationship with you by getting to know you. I daydreamed about you taking me fishing.
I called you first when I got my firearms license and purchased

my first handgun.
You took the time to talk to me about the importance of gun safety.
We spoke about you taking me horseback riding.
I am disappointed in myself that I allowed you to just talk.
Yes, a large part of the reason that I flew home was to cultivate a relationship with you and to have you get to know me.

I daydreamed about you flying up North to see me and me showing you around town.
I called you each time that I passed both of my real estate licensing exams and when I closed on my first client sale.
You took the time to talk to me about maximizing my time with clients who are qualified, approved, and ready to move.
We spoke about going to the gun range together.
I am disappointed in myself that I allowed you to just talk.
Yes, a large part of the reason that I flew home to see you was to convince you to cultivate a genuine relationship with your son.
I tried to convince you to talk to him and to hear him out without having your ego in your front pocket.
I tried to convince you to show him patience and understanding.
I tried to convince you to love him unconditionally and to sincerely apologize to him.
I am disappointed in myself that I allowed you to just talk.
I dreamed of having my father in my life.
However, you and I both know that the primary reason that I flew home to see you was because of Jr. I knew that my nephew was in trouble. I had no actual knowledge, my spirit simply felt it. I told you that last I heard, he was still away, but every ounce of my intuition told me that whether in or out, his time here was going to be cut short. I had no idea how little time he had left. I flew home to see you in September of 2019. Jr was taken from us in December of 2019.

Man, 18, fatally shot in North Philadelphia Wednesday morning

fox29.com - 11 minutes ago

Nightmares;

It did not have to happen.
Our family lived in that
environment.
Our family was never of that
environment.
Our family was aware of that
environment.
Our family did not take part in
that environment.
Our family has always been
1 degree away from many
headline news stories.
Our family became a headline news story.
As I think back on all of it now, it is hard for me to believe.
I am only mindful of it all because my mind is full of it all.

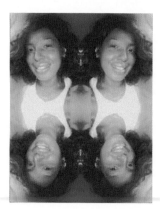

2020 Vision;

2020 started off promising
2020 then became a world wind for me.
2020 took Kobe.
2020 housed an enormous amount of
closed chapters and opened doors.
2020 was full of worldly tragedy coupled
with personal triumph.
2020 peeled back the curtains while pulling
out layers of empathy.

2020 taught me even more patience, grace and the importance of loving others as you love yourself.
2020 cemented my personal relationship with God and my complete trust in my faith.
2020 reinforced "No" being my complete sentence, I am grateful for all of it.
2020 showed me that I have one more door to close, the door leading to you.
I see clearly.

In December of 2019, when my nephew passed away, I got the call at 2am. I called you immediately. I remember afterwards being up for almost two days straight on the telephone with tons of family, family friends, and childhood friends. I was stressed out, drained and exhausted. That time period still feels like I dreamt it. I had some tough decisions to make. You gave me one piece of advice that turned out to be the only thing that I ever needed from you and I do not take advice from anyone. Especially not from someone whom I wouldn't want to trade lives with. I always loved who I was and I am in love with who I am becoming. So, again, I don't take others advice, I don't want to trade my life for anyone else's.

However, you said something to me that I did apply. You told me to stop putting gas in broken down cars. You explained to me that all of this time I have been putting gas in the tanks of cars that I knew were broken down, just so that they could drive a few short blocks. Those same cars would go empty and I'd fill up the tanks again, at my own expense, while watching them break down. Then I'd put a little more gas in the tank hoping that maybe this time around, the car would make it to the repair shop, nope here it comes again, broken down. Each time leaving me depleted and empty, without any reciprocal replenishing.

See sometimes I only understand life through analogies. No one can advise me or decide for me what's best for my life. No one knows or understands, better than I do, what my heart's truest desires and needs are, so I don't give anyone that power. It turns out that you were actually right. I applied that advice and I'm happy with my decision. I'm no longer filling up anyone's tank including yours, Sir. "Every tub has to stand on its own bottom." - Ms. Lauryn Hill

You are not absolved of your responsibility, Sir. You do not get a pass. You must answer to your creator. We have a family legacy of broken children making permanent decisions of marrying, divorcing, co-parenting, and single parent households. We have a family legacy of broken children making permanent decisions based on temporary emotions that affect countless lives. When do you take responsibility? There is a common ground if you take the position of a father who abandoned his children. That is the only priority.

Your Firstborn Son;
You loved his mother.
You created him.
He was born on your birthday.
You molded who he has become.
He tried to make you proud.
You moved on to chapter two.
You disappointed him.
He has become you.

As I was driving up and down in the South, I listened to a ton of music. I chose to listen to songs that helped me in processing my emotions. It brought back the nostalgia of my formative years. In Columbia, I listened to Lalah Hathaway's self-titled debut album. That is the one album that shaped our summer of 1992. There is a special story with a special meaning behind it that I have never shared with anyone. You remember that year was the last time that you drove up North to see us. That summer was the last time that I actually laid eyes on you before now. I was 15 years old.

You drove up to attend my brother's high school graduation to see him walk across the stage. He was so proud to have his father in the audience. Afterwards, we gathered at my grandmother's house for our usual family celebration of food and laughter. Later that evening, he and I both drove back to South Carolina with you. I was spending the entire summer there then flying back home once school started back. My brother enrolled in college and would be staying with you while attending

school. He only lasted about one year. I do not know the full extent of what happened. I have heard stories.

My brother decided to move back up North after that experience. We never talked much about it. Later on, he enlisted in the Air Force. My mother made it crystal clear to both of us very early on that we would figure out our own paths in life. She would not support us nor would she enable us as adults. However, our mother was always fully supportive in whatever our vision was. She allowed us to make mistakes while fully trusting us never to stray too far away from how we were raised yet, granting us room and grace to fall and get back up.

"Train up a child in the way he should go, and when he is old, he will not depart from it" Proverbs 22:6.

I, too, went to university right after high school. I went off to the suburbs of New York attending Long Island University. I thought that I wanted to live in the city that never sleeps. I quickly discovered that it was not for me. I completed one year. I retained my credits for that one year but I'm embarrassed to admit that I still have student loan debt that I do not wish to pay. The college campus life simply was not for me. I am a nerd and a socially awkward, introverted loner.

I have countless fond memories from that one year at school. That one year defined my independence. My college roommate assigned to my dorm room never showed up for school. For whatever odd reason, the University never assigned anyone else to my room; that year was incredible. I had a boyfriend back home that I was missing terribly. He'd take the New Jersey Transit Train back and forth to come up to see me on weekends. He had his own place, so on many weekends I'd sneak back home to see him. My mother would have absolutely no idea that I was in town. Eventually the time spent with him at his house would increase from Friday through Sunday to Thursday to Tuesday then full weeks at a time. I would go completely M.I.A.

There were no cell phones back then, so no one could reach me. My mother would call my dorm non-stop, leaving message after message threatening to force me to leave school if I didn't get it together. I'd befriended a girl named Yessenia. She was single so she asked if my boyfriend had any friends that he could introduce her to. He hooked her up with his brother and they fell in love. Eventually, all four of us formed our own world that felt far more important than college studies. I remember him and I continuing to date for a few years after I'd completed that one year of school and returned back home to figure out my next move. He and I have the shared experience of watching the Iconic Mike Tyson vs. Evander Holyfield fight. We saw the ear biting incident live, in real time.

Those days were epic.

My dorm room became the chill spot. In addition to Yessenia, I'd also made friends with some of the other girls on campus. We'd all cut class together playing Monopoly and smoking weed all day long. I'm extremely competitive, so we'd play for hours on end. If I wasn't winning the game I was not satisfied. I had to be the one who owned all of the prime Real Estate that there was to have. We'd play until someone went totally bust. If it looked as if someone else was going to win I'd flip the board over forcing us to start again. To this day, I have no idea how I eventually pulled it together in the 25th hour in order to pass all of my courses and gain my full credits but I wouldn't trade anything for it.

I now call that work-life balance.

During the summer of 1992, my brother and I used to steal your car; your stick shift Volkswagen Dune Buggy. My brother almost burnt your clutch out on more occasions than I can recall. Every chance that we got, we stole your car, we'd joy ride around town. We would be certain to remember to match the gas in the car before we parked it back in your driveway so that you would not notice. Now that I think about it, I don't even recall how we got gas money; neither of us had a job that summer.

My brother was resilient; he taught himself how to drive a stick shift simply by execution. He got better at it every day, ironically, I was terrified that you would find out, but I was his wingman, and that was my big brother, so every day I went along for the ride.

One day we went to the Richland Mall to buy some music. We walked the mall, talking, and laughing while reminiscing. This was way back when they had music podium stations set up with headphones. You could listen to samples of music before you purchased the cd. We decided on Lalah Hathaway. We could not wait to blast our cd in your car as we hurried home to make sure that we got there before you and Jenny got off work.

That Lalah Hathaway album became our forever soundtrack; our throwback soundtrack to the summer of 1992. Over the years as we've migrated into our own lives and have lived our own individual experiences, through our disagreements and distance that album always unites us.

Throughout that summer, we drove to our old neighborhoods trying to locate our old friends. We drove to our last house on Dartmore Lane while my brother would tell me once again how he felt all those years ago when we were put out of our home. Over the years he has told me countless times about the pain he felt. I would always patiently listen as if he were telling me the story for the first time. He told me that on that day, all that he wanted to do was go home and fix him a bowl of Butter Pecan ice cream with Ritz Crackers. He'd been thinking about it all day at school and could not wait until the school bell rang. As we neared our house, I remember being confused about what was happening. My first thought was that maybe our mother had gotten home from work early and decided to have a yard sale so that our lights wouldn't get cut off anymore. Yard sales were a staple around town. My mother had a passion for them. As we got older, we realized that our mother had become a hoarder of junk and we secretly nicknamed her Fred Sanford. It then became our running family joke.

We became latch key kids after your divorce. We walked home together from school daily. On that last day, we saw all of our furniture sitting outside on the lawn, strewn up and down our driveway. All of the locks had been changed, so our door keys wouldn't work in any of the locks. I remember my brother saying that he saw the half gallon of butter pecan ice cream sitting outside melting and he just sat staring at it until our mother had gotten home. I used to play with letters and make words on a magnetic stand-up chalkboard. My white chalkboard was in the grass right outside of my bedroom window. I remember seeing the letter K in red laying next to it. I don't remember much after that, like where we spent the night or even where our dogs were. Trauma causes major memory lapse.

I have decided to begin the process of mourning you right now. I will not wait until I get a telephone call in the middle of the night telling me that you passed away. You refuse to see yourself or deal with yourself. Remaining in contact with you is not healthy for me. Don't you know that something is wrong with you? There is no man alive, walking on God's green earth who is mentally healthy, stable, whole, or emotionally mature who discards his children, grandchildren, and great grandchildren.

It is so easy for you to point your finger blaming everyone else for everything that's "wrong" with you and "wrong" in your life. That way, you get to completely remove yourself from the equation. If you are not the common denominator, you have zero responsibility for righting any of your wrongs. My mother was "wrong" for leaving you. We are "wrong" for thinking that you should reach out to us. We are also "wrong" for feeling like our father should want to cultivate a relationship with us. Where do you hold any liability, Sir?

Living a Lie;
The lies are so much easier for you to live.
The lies are so much easier for you to tell.
The lies are easier for you to digest.
The lies are soothing to you, they are warm, cozy, comfortable, and all too familiar.
Blame-shifting is far more entertaining for you.
Blame-shifting is less pressure on yourself.
Blame-shifting requires zero work or personal accountability.

If something is always wrong everywhere else and in everyone else, you escape all responsibility.

If something is always wrong outside of yourself, then you don't need to do anything at all inside of yourself in order to change your own narrative.

If something else is broken and you do not recognize that you are also broken, how can you lead a family?

If you refuse to do the work that is required to begin healing the broken parts of you, how can you have healthy dialogues, friendships, relationships or a marriage?

If there is no one there to hold up a mirror and if you refuse to look in your mirror, then you have no work to do.

It gets really comfortable to coast through life dancing. You are constantly toe to toe with like minds that will keep you on the dance floor of dysfunction.

All you have to do is keep the beat going and keep on dancing.

Crystal;

I must make myself crystal clear.
You were always where I needed you to be whether you were there or not there.
As I look back now, I am incredibly grateful that you were not a part of our lives.
Thank God she left you.
Our glass was always half full.
You would have ruined us.

I Wonder;

I wonder how my step brothers Brian, Charlton and Andrew really feel about you, what they must be afraid to say.
I wonder why Andrew is really living in your attic, where my brother and I used to play as kids.
I wonder how my step sister, Delois, really feels about you.
I wonder if you realize that you never played an active

part in her upbringing and you've now successfully traumatized her all over again since you stopped communicating with her.

I wonder what you are not telling me about you and Jenny's marriage.

I wonder why Jenny never once answered the house telephone when I would call.

I wonder why it seems that she's afraid of you or why she is never there in the house with you.

I wonder why she was never already there when I was at home visiting with you, why it seemed that her random pop-ups were prompted by a telephone call initiated by Andrew or why I never heard her voice in the background whenever you and I spoke on the telephone.

I wonder why you were going to the store buying household supplies and toiletries if your marriage is still intact.

I wonder why you do not have great stories to share with me about you and Jenny taking amazing vacations and traveling the world together.

I wonder why it took you months to go up to Rockhill to see your grandson, Colton, Charlton's firstborn son.

I wonder if the boys think that you are extremely judgmental about their life decisions or about their choices in their spouses, the same way that I feel that you are.

I wonder if you know that marrying Jenny did not necessarily mean that you made a bad choice.

I wonder if you know that it's ok to

not have the picture perfect marriage or family structure, as most people don't.

I wonder if you know that none of that makes you a failure.

I wonder if you know that I believe that you tried.

I wonder if you know that I see you.

I wonder if you know that I can see through you and that is why you avoid me.

I wonder when or if you will forgive and free yourself from your self-inflicted chains.

I wonder when the disconnect happened between you and my mother.

I wonder why you guys broke up in high school.

I wonder what you said to get her back.

I wonder if you no longer desired her after she got pregnant with my brother, gained weight then gave birth.

I wonder if, in your eyes, she was no longer your perfect ideal wife physically.

I wonder if you lost your attraction to her after she got pregnant for the second time, with me, after her body really got soft, after her breasts began to sag, after she smelled like our dirty diapers and vomit.

I wonder if you know that the former is what marriage and life partnership is truly about.

I wonder if perhaps being a housewife with two babies and no family support became overwhelming to her.

I wonder if she was too overwhelmed to properly balance being a wife first, then a mother.

I wonder if the many nights of tears that you made her cry ever even affected you.

I wonder if you became resentful of her because you knew that her wings could not be clipped, you knew that she was so much more than a wife and a mother.

I wonder if you were aware of her greatest potential long before she ever was.

I wonder if you always knew that her light would shine bright but you just couldn't stand to see it.

My mother's favorite cake was coconut with white icing. Her favorite ice cream was Butter Pecan. Her favorite nuts were whole walnuts, oven roasted peanuts or wet boiled peanuts. She loved to cook and was amazing at it. Some of her favorite meals were stewed tomatoes with okra over rice, whole Red Snapper fish with the head on it, and canned fried Salmon. She taught me many of those recipes. She loved to pop popcorn on the stove, in a cast iron skillet, from whole kernels. She bought me my first cast iron skillet. She sent me flowers on Valentine's day. She loved great love stories on film. She introduced me to "The Bridges of Madison County". We grew up as a family watching "The Cosby Show" and Micheal Jackson music video premieres, our favorite was Thriller. The day that

Princess Diana lost her life she and I sat at home watching the tragedy together along with the aftermath as it unfolded live on television. She too was extremely competitive. She loved playing cards and she taught me how to gamble at casinos. We spent a lot of time in Atlantic City together. Her sisters were her best friends, her favorite as you know, was my Aunt Mary. Her mother, my Grandmother Sarah Simon, was her muse.

My mother's favorite gospel song was "The Question Is" by the Winans followed by "Tomorrow". On days when I cannot stop thinking of her, I play it repeatedly in my home. Her favorite secular rap song was "All Around The World" by Jay-Z followed by "Dear Mama" by Tupac. She was in love with the instrumentation. We used to laugh hysterically when she would blast that song by Jay-Z in our home and dance like no one's business while singing at the top of her lungs. I do the same exact thing while listening to music when I am at home alone. I probably annoy my neighbors with my out of tune squealing. We were shocked the first time that we discovered that she too loved Jay-Z. This is a woman who grew up in the deep south, rooted in southern culture, raised in church listening to gospel music and she also adored Motown artists.

My mother's favorite vacation cocktail was virgin Piña Coladas. She epitomized class, and she loved to laugh. My mother's favorite color was purple. Her favorite movie was "The Color Purple", that movie is our family favorite. We've watched that movie as a family over and over again. I've seen it on my own so many times that I've lost count. Our grandfather's old juke joint along with all of the festivities embody exactly what is depicted in the movie. The setting, the times, those unspoken rules and the way of life depicted in that film is exactly how she grew up, we were witness to the majority of it.

I closed on my first real estate deal on her birthday, July 20, 2020. Just five short months after obtaining my New Jersey Real Estate license. I intentionally pushed extremely hard to meet that closing date. Everyone involved in the transaction was on board, gung-ho and fully supportive but they had no idea of the magnitude. I never thought that I could resign from Corporate America after almost two decades, speaking the language of Telecom within multiple departments, to enter into an industry that I know nothing about, learning to speak an entirely different language.

The team did not know why I pushed so hard to close the sale on that date. Even after I explained it to them they didn't quite grasp the magnitude. When I called you that evening, to tell you all about it, you didn't get it either. On that day, I wore a flowing white summer dress with purple flowers all over it to honor her. I felt like "The Color Purple" movie characters Ms. Ceily, Ms. Shug and Ms. Sophia simultaneously morphed into one being. I felt alive again.

I surrender it all now, becoming fully aware that sometimes in life no one else will ever really understand why such small things are actually monumental to me.

I now envision you as the disgruntled character Mr., shuffling to get your affairs in order. I could be wrong about the latter. I'm ok with that too.

I Wonder No More;
I used to wonder what your favorite cake was.
I used to wonder what your favorite meal was.
I used to wonder what your favorite song was.
I used to wonder what your favorite movie was.
I used to wonder what your favorite color was.
I used to wonder what your favorite hobbies were.
I used to wonder what your favorite cocktail beverage was.
I no longer care about any of that, curiosity killed the cat.
I focus on myself, I no longer wonder.

I Want the Truth;
I now wonder if you can feel the ice water running through your own veins.
I now wonder how many affairs you have had during your marriage to my mother.
I now wonder how many affairs you have had during your marriage to Jenny.
I now wonder if you know that I know that cheating is a choice. A one-time cheater is a serial cheater. A cheater is a liar and a liar is a thief.
I now wonder if Jenny has discovered that you are not

the man whom she thought that you were.
I wonder if Jenny now knows that you are not willing to grow in and fight for your marriage.
I wonder if she too has now discovered that you simply want things your way or no way at all.
I now wonder if Jenny and the boys feel that they are circling in your universe.
I now wonder what it truly looks like if anyone dares to color outside of your chalk lines, how they've personally experienced your wrath.
I now wonder if Jenny lives with Charlton, his wife and your grandson Colton in Rockhill, as everyone, on your side of my family, assumes.
I now wonder if you know what we all really know about you.
I now wonder why you continue to lie to me by painting a picture of a happy, successful family unit while everyone seems to be afraid of you.
I now wonder why Andrew is sleeping in your attic.

You have to lie because you have to be right. You have to have made the right decision with chapter two, right? I wonder why you try so hard to force it to look like it's functioning. It's because it has to work, right? Why is Andrew in the attic? That's not even your style of parenting. You would never have allowed us to live in your attic as adults. Where is Jenny?

I could go on, I chose to stop there.

As a child in summer camp, at Camp William Penn, on my first day, I jumped off of a diving board into 12 feet of water. The concept of actually knowing how to swim had never entered my mind. I went straight to the bottom of the pool, almost drowning. My brother stood by and watched in horror as I had to be rescued and resuscitated.

I never allowed that incident to stop me or force me to develop a fear of water. I now know how to swim. Years later, as a 16-year-old, I went back and worked at Camp William Penn, as a Senior Camp Counselor. I lied about my age on the job application. I impressed the camp director so much during the interview that he gave me the job. All camp counselors had to move there for the entire summer. The staff needed to be sure that we would conduct ourselves accordingly. The senior camp counselor positions were only allocated to 18-year-olds. I remember the director and I making a pact, he emphatically told me not to reveal to anyone that I was underage. I have been shot in the face with a BB gun, while defending my brother. I have been hit by a car and thrown 15 feet in the air. I fell off my bicycle once and was punctured in my leg by the whole kickstand. I have been stabbed in the knee with a number 2 pencil. You weren't there for any of it but I survived.

I have been in multiple car accidents, one that almost claimed my life in July of 2015. As I was rushing to the hospital, to see my mother, who had been rushed to the hospital, I passed out behind the wheel of my car. I collided head-on into oncoming traffic. Thankfully there were no major injuries or fatalities. I totaled my brand new car that I'd just purchased two weeks prior. Two weeks after that I purchased the exact same car. My insurance company handled the rest. I spent the night in jail. I have been paying for it ever since. You weren't there for any of it but I survived.

I have survived physically and emotionally abusive relationships. One incident, in particular, is a story that still haunts me today. It has changed the very fabric of my being and how I deal with men. It has changed my vetting process by checking the level of emotional well being, stability, and maturity before proceeding forward. It has taught me a new level of compassion and empathy for hurt people. It has taught me just how damaging and dangerous it can be to be with a partner who is jealous of your achievements as well as your light, especially when they have none of their own, only darkness. It has taught me not to date men who are not equally yoked. It has taught me that not knowing who I am, settling for less, and not allowing my intuition to guide me could have cost me my life. It has taught me that jealousy and envy from frenemies or a life partner, as well as their denial, or lack of ownership of their own demons can be projected onto me through the rage of sour bitterness and defeat and how that shows up as sabotage, aggression, verbal and physical abuse. Does any of this sound familiar, Sir? You weren't there for any of it but I survived.

I was a top seller and a top achiever in Corporate America. Being the best by exceeding in sales and service is in my DNA. In 2005, I exceeded sales for a product called DSL. DSL was implemented around the time that faster internet service was in high demand. The acronym was short for Digital Subscriber Line service. It was the first of its kind, serving as high-speed internet over traditional hard wired telephone landline service. I won an all expenses paid trip to the Grammy Awards in Los Angeles, California. I was elated, however, the expenses were fully paid by my company, solely for me. We had the option of bringing a guest but we were individually responsible for our guests expenses. It was Valentine's weekend, so naturally, I wanted to share the experience with the man that I was dating at the time. I never told him this, but I paid for his airfare and I told him to pack his bags.

He was someone that I should never have been dating. My mother never approved of him or his lifestyle. He did not fit into my family of green square southerners with our corny family traditions of religion, love and togetherness. He was never comfortable and barely spent any time around them. It was a work trip, so we had a host of conferences and functions to attend that were solely for company employees. There was plenty of off time as well for us to explore

Hollywood, to be left at our own leisure.

The trip started off rocky. As soon as we landed in California, I quickly learned that the airline had lost my luggage. Not his, he had all of his bags. I had nothing, not a toothbrush, a t-shirt or even a stitch of undergarments. Back then I was packing for vacations a lot differently. That one trip changed the way that I now pack. I now load a ton of essentials and roll several outfits into my carry on bags just in case.

Once I learned that I had no clothing for a 3 day 2 night vacation, my brain went into the overdrive of survival mode. I had to figure it out and figure it out fast. I had a work function to attend the night that we landed. I only had a couple of hours to prepare. I immediately googled the nearest mall. I found a Bloomingdale's store inside of a local mall. I shopped for new clothes and all of the essentials that I would need while he sat by stewing in a chair, in the corner of the department store.

I made out pretty good; the only small problem was that I could not find a replacement dress that I was satisfied with to attend the Grammy Award Ceremony. We landed on a Friday evening. The Grammy Awards Ceremony was that Sunday. In my missing luggage was my special dress, throw and shoes to match that I was dying to wear. At home, I'd searched and searched for the perfect dress to fit my then voluptuous body, full of curves. When you are a woman of a particular weight, it is not that easy to find clothing that you are comfortable in that also flatters your body shape. I was optimistic yet bummed out. He did not add any light to the end of the tunnel. He complained and grumbled the entire time. I have learned through life's experience that narcissistic people never have anything nice or kind to say. I have learned that they find a problem for every problem and that they find a way to enjoy adding stress to any stressful situation. Despite that, I was optimistic that before Sunday, the airline would call to tell me that they'd found my luggage and that I would be able to wear my special dress.

After a couple of hours of shopping, we finally checked into our hotel. I quickly showered and changed clothes to attend my work event. The event was fun-filled, I met fellow employees from all over the country. There was one management employee, a woman named Annette, that I knew personally from my local office who was also on the trip. When we got to the venue that Friday evening, they had a red carpet rolled out for us, a buffet, and top shelf drinks were flowing. They had celebrity impersonators dressed up in drag, and we had an amazing night! There was a Cher impersonator, Whoppi Goldberg and countless others. We socialized, we danced, ate, drank, and we laughed for hours.

Apparently, he was still stewing inside of the hotel room by himself. I remember not telling him that he could not attend the event until the last minute. I remember telling him to go out, explore California, and have fun, but he was livid. I got back to the hotel room, and all hell broke loose. I had such a good time that evening that I came bursting into the hotel room with pure joy and excitement. I could not wait to tell him all about my night. I know now that he was not interested in hearing about me having a good time.

Dark Energies;
Narcissists are never interested in hearing good news about others.
Narcissists never care to see others happy.
Narcissists are adamant about painting a dark picture of others because their insides are dark, especially when they have spoken about you in horrible ways, having tried to paint a false picture of you.
Narcissists will do everything in their power to try to beat the light out of you, by beating you into submission.
Narcissists exhale darkness.

I remember being at my work event and thinking to myself that once I got back to the hotel, I would suggest to him that we could venture out together, maybe find some late night eatery, or just walk and talk while exploring California, but none of that happened. My excitement quickly turned into confusion. He was so angry with me, I could not understand where his rage was stemming from.

The airline lost my luggage, not his. I had to spend money that I did not anticipate spending, in order to recoup a full wardrobe, even purchasing an extra suitcase to fly it all back home in. He did not contribute to any of that and I did not ask him to. I was still trying my best to make the most of it by not allowing it to phase me, but his spirit was so dark that I could not hold it in anymore. I asked him what in the world was wrong with him and why the hell was he acting like this. That is when he lost it. I was standing up by the television, he was seated in a chair next to the sliding glass doors that led out onto our hotel balcony. I am still in disbelief about what happened next. He stood up and cocked his hand back, then brought it back forward hitting me across the face so hard that he then threw me through the sliding glass doors right out onto our balcony. I remember laying there in shock. I gathered myself, got up and I walked back into the hotel room. I remember turning back to look at the spot where I landed. I was staring blankly at the broken glass as well as my blood. At that exact moment, a piece of jagged glass dropped right down into the spot where I was laying. I remember thinking that if I had not gotten up when I did, that the glass could have sliced my neck open. I remember thinking that if the hotel room had no balcony at all, I would not be here today to tell this story.

Battered Wife Syndrome;
I remember calling security, them coming to our room and me lying to them.
I remember me telling security that I fell.
I remember security looking on the floor of the hotel room and seeing where my shoe had come off.
I remember watching security notice the distance between where I was standing and where I ended up.

I remember the security guard telling me that it is humanly impossible to simply fall from one side of the room to the next, falling straight through thick sliding glass doors of a 5-star hotel room.
I remember my fear as one of the security guards assessed the situation by looking at his body language as well as mine.
I remember security asking me why he wasn't trying to console me or help me.
I remember the security guard pulling me to the side, asking me if I wanted to press charges against him and have him put in jail.
I remember the other security guard stepping out onto the balcony, sifting through the glass, finding my diamond earring and placing it in my hands.
I remember that my hands were shaking uncontrollably.
I remember my tears and my terror.
I remember whispering in the bathroom to the security guard.
I remember being cut up and bruised but ok.
I remember telling security that I was on a work trip.
I remember telling security that I was only 5 years in with my company and I did not know what would happen to me, if they found out.
I remember asking security to simply put us in a new room.
I remember telling the security guard that I would figure the rest out later.
I remember that he committed attempted murder and I lied to protect him.
I remember choosing to not ruin him by putting him in jail.
I remembered that he was ruined long before we ever met.
I remember the red flags that I chose to ignore.
I remember being an enabler.
I remember blaming myself.
I discovered that I had Battered Wife Syndrome.

I later confessed to Annette. I told her everything about what happened that night and ironically she too, was having difficulties with her, then husband, whom she had also brought on the trip. I remember her talking me through that experience and she and I hanging out together on the trip afterwards. I remember she and I later finding a way to laugh about both of them and how damaged a man would have to be inside to do that to a woman whom he said he loved and to think nothing of it.

When a narcissist cannot win by attempting to make you feel less than, they become abusive. When a narcissist cannot win at their attempts to assassinate your character, they try to kill you. A narcissist wants you as dead as they are inside. They are never the problem; it is always you. They are never genuinely apologetic. "I'm sorry", always comes with either a preface or an addendum. Both the former and the latter find a way to point blame toward their victims.

The following piece isn't mine, I found it online.

> **A Narcissist's Prayer;**
> *That did not happen, and if it did, it was not that bad.*
> *And if it was, it was not a big deal.*
> *And if it is, that is not my fault.*
> *And if it was, I didn't mean it.*
> *And if I did, you deserved it.*

There are no apologies or accountability. Does any of this sound familiar to you, Sir? I survived that trauma without you there to protect me, so what do I really need you for now. That is not a question. I gave you a fair chance. Are we even in your will? Do you not think that you owe us anything at all?

Oh, by the way, the airline did indeed call me to tell me that they'd found my luggage. It was late that Saturday evening. I had to skip out on one of my work functions to take a cab back to the airport and pick up my bags. I was able to wear my special dress to the 2005 Grammy Award Ceremony. I had an incredible time with my fellow co-workers. He did not attend.

After we flew back home, without incident I swiftly changed the locks of my home, politely packed all of his belongings and placed them all outside on the front steps, in 7 trash bags.

The last thing that I will say is this. My brother wanted to know why you did not name him a Jr. I made it my business to ask you. I believe and I felt that you told me the truth when you answered. You said that you never liked your name Charlie, so you did not want to name him after you. You also said that because he was your firstborn son, you could not in good conscience name any of the three boys that came after him, a Jr. You said that you wanted us all to have strong names and Charlton was as close as you would allow.

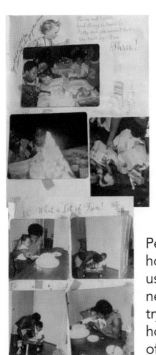

I was extremely proud of you for being present-minded enough to not cause my brother that type of additional hurt. When I asked you about my name and where it came from, things got a tad bit sticky. I always knew why my nickname became a staple. From a very young age; both you and my mother shortened my first name with my nickname. You called me Ken while she felt that it was too masculine calling me Kim instead. Even today, my full first name sounds foreign to me. I only use it in professional settings, when I am forced to. Once I received my Pennsylvania Real Estate license I figured out how to petition the state so that I could legally use my nickname. I obtained the paperwork necessary in order to do so. I'm still working on trying to do the same in my home state of New Jersey. As of today, no such workaround exists.

My mother never called me by my full first name, unless she was extremely upset with me and I did my best to try to avoid upsetting her at all costs. Any friend, family member, former co-worker or associate that has ever truly known me, calls me Kim.

My middle name is the rub. It is quite unique, I have never heard it before, I most certainly have never seen a name pronounced the way that mine is, or spelled the same. You told me that you had no idea where my middle name came from. I simply said ok and I left it at that.

I believe that it came from the Bible, the story of Abraham. I'm unable to confirm that to be totally accurate, but I wondered, have you really never realized that my middle name was derived from yours? The "C" pronounced like an "S" is an ode to her Mother Sarah. Your name is Charlie, my middle name is Cire' the "E" is pronounced as an "A".

All four letters of my middle name are in your first name.
My mother loved my name just as much as I do.
I did not have the heart to tell you.

I am praying for you Sir, and I love you with Agape love. If you want to check up on me, you can Google me. I bet you a dollar to a donut on that one. You can recruit Andrew from the attic to show you how. I was always a timid Daniel who never really spoke up for myself. I feel that I have now slain the giant known as Goliath. The only thing that I still wonder about is whether or not I am also Goliath. I wonder if the 4 year old Daniel inside of me was simply trying to fight for the now 44 year old Goliath that I have become. I'm most certainly a beautiful monster of sorts, filled with a range of emotions trying hard to gently fight for all of the other Daniels of the world.

These words were always inside of me. I did not ask for this; God gave it to me. This is always who I was, I simply had to tap in to discover myself. God is my Alpha and my Omega but not in any traditional, "Only on Sunday morning" sense.

He spared me, I refuse to believe that it's by happenstance. I owe Him everything. You were simply the seed tasked to fertilize the egg that then created me. You can choose to remain on the sidelines. Your job with me is finished. I'm now an outlier for purpose.

"Before I formed thee in the belly, I knew thee and I ordained thee a prophet unto the nations;" Jeremiah 1:5

This is my purpose. I am not asking you or anyone else for permission. - Your youngest daughter, Kim Cire'.

ACKNOWLEDGEMENT

Life is comprised of a series of moments.

Both the good and the bad times, all of your ups and your downs are inevitable.

How you choose to process your life's story by applying your own healthy personal perspective is your gift.

I pray that you use your gifts wisely.

ABOUT THE AUTHOR

Kim Jacobs was born in South Carolina and is truly a Southern Gal at heart.

This book was born out of necessity; it started off as a simple letter that she decided to write to her father after the decline of their reconnection. It outlines her healing in real time. Kim decided to unpack all of her painful trauma by examining it in the healthiest way possible in order to apply the proper perspective. Kim describes in full detail the ups and the downs that she experienced throughout the Covid-19 Pandemic of 2020 as it relates to her severed Father-Daughter connection.

Kim has rebranded herself as Phoenix On Purpose and has Trademarked her personal Brand ~ Purpose NOT Permission™.

Kim is passionate about animals, travel, creative arts, film, self-development, reading, writing, bodies of water, spontaneous adventures and walking barefoot in nature.

Kim is a licensed Realtor® in New Jersey and Pennsylvania as well as a New Jersey Mobile Notary Public and licensed New Jersey Insurance Producer.

Kim is now a writer by trade. Writing was always her gift and her passion. She also performs live poetry via spoken word, has a YouTube Channel and a Podcast Streaming now on all available Podcast Stations.

Kim is conquering all of her fears by becoming…

THEN

NOW

DEDICATION